URBAN RAIL TRANSIT:
Its Economics and Technology

OTHER PUBLICATIONS FROM
THE M.I.T.–HARVARD JOINT CENTER
FOR URBAN STUDIES

EDWARD C. BANFIELD and JAMES Q. WILSON, *City Politics in America: An Interpretation.* Harvard University Press** and The M.I.T. Press, 1963. $6.95.

JOHN E. BURCHARD and OSCAR HANDLIN, eds., *The Historian and the City.* The M.I.T. Press* and Harvard University Press, 1963, $7.50.

NATHAN GLAZER and DANIEL PATRICK MOYNIHAN, *Beyond the Melting Pot.* The M.I.T. Press* and Harvard University Press, 1963. $5.95.

CHARLES HAAR, *Law and Land: Anglo-American Planning Practice.* Harvard University Press** and The M.I.T. Press, 1963. $7.50.

KEVIN LYNCH, *The Image of the City.* The M.I.T. Press* and Harvard University Press, 1960. $5.50.

LLOYD RODWIN, *Housing and Economic Progress.* The M.I.T. Press* and Harvard University Press, 1961. $7.50.

SAM B. WARNER, JR., *Streetcar Suburbs.* Harvard University Press** and The M.I.T. Press, 1962. $6.50.

MORTON and LUCIA WHITE, *The Intellectual Versus the City: From Thomas Jefferson to Frank Lloyd Wright.* Harvard University Press** and The M.I.T. Press, 1962. $5.50.

DONALD APPLEYARD, KEVIN LYNCH, and JOHN R. MYER, *The View from the Road.* The M.I.T. Press,* 1964. $5.95.

JOHN DELAFONS, *Land Use Controls in the United States.* Harvard University Press,** 1962. $3.50.

MARTHA DERTHICK, *City Politics in Washington, D. C.* Harvard University Press,** 1962. $4.00.

RICHARD L. MEIER, *A Communications Theory of Urban Growth.* The M.I.T. Press,* 1962. $4.50.

GEORGE STERNLIEB, *The Future of the Downtown Department Store.* Harvard University Press,** 1962. $4.00.

RAYMOND VERNON, *The Myth and Reality of Our Urban Problems.* Harvard University Press,** 1962. $3.00.

ROBERT A. WOODS and ALBERT J. KENNEDY, *The Zone of Emergence.* Harvard University Press,** 1962. $4.00.

Order through your bookseller, or

*Available from THE M·I·T PRESS, Cambridge 42, Massachusetts

**Available from HARVARD UNIVERSITY PRESS, Cambridge 38, Mass.

URBAN RAIL TRANSIT:
Its Economics and Technology

A. Scheffer Lang
Richard M. Soberman

Published for
The Joint Center for Urban Studies
of the Massachusetts Institute of Technology and Harvard University

by
THE M.I.T. PRESS
Massachusetts Institute of Technology
Cambridge, Massachusetts

The Joint Center for Urban Studies, a cooperative venture of
the Massachusetts Institute of Technology and Harvard University,
was founded in 1959 to do research on urban and regional problems.
Participants have included scholars from the fields of architecture,
business, engineering, city planning, economics, history, law,
philosophy, political science, and sociology. This monograph is
one of a series in which the Joint Center presents some of its
findings. The Joint Center also sponsors a series of books.

Library of Congress Catalog Card Number 63-23379

Printed in the United States of America

PREFACE

A large part of this work involved the collection of data, during the course of which many discussions were held with people actively engaged in planning and operating rail transit systems. The list of those who contributed in this way is long.   J. N. Jaboris, George Krambles, and C. B. North of the Chicago Transit Authority; Donald Hyde and George Ihnat of the Cleveland Transit System; William Lassow, R. G. Welch, H. V. Scherrer, and Alan Fawcett of the New York City Transit Authority;   and W. F. Irvin,   L. W. Bardsley, James Field,   and J. Armour of the Toronto Transit Commission were particularly generous of their time. W. L. Sheppard and L. F. Reynolds of the Budd Company and W. C. Wheeler of the St. Louis Car Company were also extremely helpful in providing assistance on the subject of rail transit equipment.

The authors are particularly indebted to Mr. E. L. Tennyson, Transit Operations Engineer for the City of Philadelphia,   for his patience in reading and commenting on almost the entire manuscript during its various stages of development. We are also indebted to our colleague, Martin Wohl, and to George W. Anderson and W. S. Rainville of the American Transit Association for their help at different points of our study.

The study was sponsored by the Joint Center for Urban Studies of the Massachusetts Institute of Technology and Harvard University. The continuing support offered by its former director, Professor Martin Meyerson, long after the study was scheduled for completion, is gratefully acknowledged.

November 1963   A. S. Lang
Cambridge, Massachusetts   Richard M. Soberman

CONTENTS

LIST OF TABLES

LIST OF ILLUSTRATIONS

xi

URBAN RAIL TRANSIT:
ITS ECONOMICS AND TECHNOLOGY

Chapter 1

INTRODUCTION

This book attempts to fill some of the gap that has existed in the literature on rail transit[1] transportation since F. W. Doolittle wrote his Studies in the Cost of Urban Transportation in 1916. Doolittle's book was written during a time when almost all urban rail transit facilities were privately owned. It was, in fact, essentially a handbook for prospective investors in urban rail transportation companies. Public action then was largely restricted to ensuring that these privately owned companies did not take undue advantage of their monopoly positions. Since Doolittle's time, however, the role of urban rail transit has changed significantly.

Today, the profit-making possibilities of rail transit systems are remote from the minds of those concerned with urban transportation. Public intervention which was once regulatory or restraining has become largely a sustaining action, and public authorities have taken over practically all rail transit operations in our major cities. Local governments have generally taken this action when it became apparent that transit operations could no longer be sustained by private entrepreneurial effort alone. The administration and financing of existing (and future) rail transit systems has thus raised major problems in many cities.

---

[1] We shall use the term rail transit throughout this book to mean a system of intra-urban passenger transportation employing single or multiple-unit electric trains supported on two-rail track and utilizing separated rights of way free of interference from other modes of transportation. If the reader chooses, he may read "rail rapid transit" for rail transit. The definition is meant, in any case, to exclude most conventional streetcar operation as well as conventional railway commuter train operation, and to focus on subway, elevated, and surface rail transit operations such as those in New York, Chicago, Philadelphia, Boston, Cleveland, and Toronto. While the definition is further meant to exclude those forms of technology which are loosely subsumed under the heading of "monorails," the reader should not overlook the strong similarities between rail transit and certain types of monorail proposals. In this regard, see H. S. D. Botzow, Monorails (New York: Simmons-Boardman Books, 1960).

3

1.1 The Experience of Recent Years

Urban highway usage has grown steadily since the end of World War II, but rail transit patronage has declined far below even its prewar levels. Figure 1.1 makes this clear. Recent indications are that this decline may have finally stopped, but the change is so slight as to seem little cause for optimism. Total rail transit patronage is still failing to keep pace with urban population growth. The causes lie in the changing nature of our cities and in the characteristics of rail transit as compared to its principal competitor, the private automobile.

In the decade 1950-1960 the total population of the 27 largest urban areas in the United States increased by nearly 25 per cent; yet

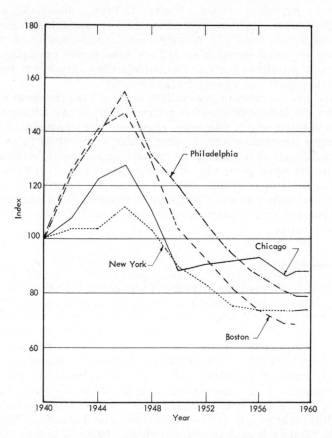

Figure 1.1. Rail rapid transit-trends of revenue passenger traffic. (Index of passengers 1940).
Source: American Transit Association.

the population of the central cities in those areas increased less than 2 per cent.[2] The resulting shift in the demand for urban transportation has been inevitable. The total number of persons entering the central business districts of our large metropolitan areas has remained more or less constant over the past 20 years, but the percentage of these trips made by automobile has increased substantially in almost every case. Those trips which have remained on the public transit systems have been confined increasingly to the rush hours alone. Although the total number of trips throughout each urban area has increased as population has increased, automobiles have absorbed the entire growth and more.[3]

As the pattern of urban decentralization has spread, travelers have not illogically shown a growing preference for the comfort, convenience, freedom from schedules, flexibility of movement, and, in some cases, lower cost of the private automobile. A seated, door-to-door trip by automobile at a cost usually underestimated by the traveler often seems preferable to a standing, nondoor-to-door trip by transit for which a cash fare must be paid. This is particularly true during off-peak hours when the trip-time disadvantage most often lies with the transit rather than the automobile ride.

The general public attitude toward transit has also affected its use. As the automobile has acquired increased importance as a symbol of social status, the social acceptability of public transit has declined. As peak-hour transit travel has become more crowded, it has seemed more demeaning to a population increasingly able to afford the admitted luxuries of an automobile. The physical deterioration and aesthetic obsolescence of their facilities have contributed further to the growing market disadvantage of many transit systems. In the face of declining patronage these same systems have often been unable to finance improvements in service which could match the growing popularity of the automobile.[4]

While transit patronage has generally declined, transit costs have

---

[2] See Wilbur Smith and Associates, Future Highways and Urban Growth, New Haven, 1961, p. 13.

[3] Ibid., p. 111 shows a 20 per cent decline in rail transit riding since 1940.

[4] Walter Oi has made a particularly penetrating analysis of the long-run shift in consumer expenditures for urban transportation. He shows that the automobile has not only increasingly displaced public transportation as an object of consumer expenditures, but it has also assumed a greater importance in consumer budgets than that which can be attributed solely to higher real incomes. See Walter Oi, The Economics of Urban Travel, Paper prepared at the Transportation Center, Northwestern University, Evanston, Illinois, 1960, pp. 119 ff.

gone up. Productivity per man-hour has improved somewhat, but
in a relatively labor-intensive industry unit labor costs have dou-
bled from 1935 to 1948 and tripled from 1935 to 1956. Declining
transit load factors, moreover, have reduced the economic efficiency of the investments in transit facilities and equipment. In contrast, because the automobile driver accounts for his labor as essentially free, the secular rise in labor costs has had little effect
on over-all private automobile operating expense.

The result is that many transit systems appear caught in a spiral
of declining traffic and a financial inability to take the steps that
might stem the decline. Public subsidy, long since instituted for
the major rail transit systems in New York and Boston, seems to
many a questionable answer in the face of growing public reliance
upon and apparent preference for the automobile. The spectacle of
bankrupt railroad commuter operations, a near cousin to urban rail
transit, seems only to vindicate the judgment of those who predict
the ultimate triumph of rubber over rail.

1.2 The Current Controversy over Transit

Paradoxically, the growing private preference for automobile
transportation confronts a growing public disaffection for it. Many
citizens who make every urban trip by car proclaim today that the
automobile is the ultimate menace to urban life; they pronounce urban man the slave of the automobile and urban culture its victim.
They suggest that in our attempts to make cities accessible (by
means of the automobile) we shall succeed only in making them un-
inhabitable.[5]

This public clamor, in which a great many professionals partici-
pate, is not without reason. The automobile has brought serious
problems for our cities. Foremost among them is its demand for
urban land. Cities with from 20 to 40 per cent of their land com-
mitted to streets and automobile parking now face (or have already
submitted to) the awesome loss of acreage that distinguishes the
construction of urban freeways.[6] While this is a problem that suburbs and satellite communities probably can live with, such removal of land from the end uses of urban life threatens to eviscerate
our central cities and destroy the very activity that highways are
designed to serve. With their capacity to attract thousands of new
vehicles into the central city each day, moreover, these freeways
increase demands for land given over to parking.

Critics add that the automobile seems to bring other forms of

---

[5] See for example, Daniel P. Moynihan, "New Roads and Urban
Chaos," The Reporter, April 14, 1960, pp. 13-20.

[6] Of course, the bulk of this street space would be required to
provide access for deliveries and pedestrians even if very extensive transit facilities were to be provided.

waste such as interminable traffic congestion, inefficient use of
fuels, and so forth. Rail transit is offered as the means whereby we
can avoid many of these problems. The rail transit boosters say
that it is quiet, clean, "efficient," and economical of land.[7] However, this view is also oversimple. Communities considering new or
improved rail transit facilities have found their capital costs in particular are very high. Whether or not rail transit can be made acceptable aesthetically also remains problematical. In fact, rail
transit is proving anything but a ready-made answer to the urban
dream. Much remains to be learned before we can understand the
true place of rail transit in the urban scheme.

1.3 Scope of Study

A growing list of proposals to build or expand rail transit facilities has become a distinctive feature of our post-World War II urban scene. These proposals have ranged from merely fanciful, un-
professional, and casual public utterances to a series of carefully
detailed technical and economic feasibility studies. In some cases
they have brought action: new subways in Cleveland and Toronto,
extensions in Chicago, construction in Montreal, and impending construction in San Francisco.

The professionals in urban transportation—city planners, civil engineers, and transit operators—have played an important role in this
renaissance of interest, but politicians, journalists, and laymen also
have been quick to suggest rail transit schemes. While much has
thus been said, too little is known about the place of rail transit in
the articulation of urban activity. Partly because the patterns of that
activity are themselves changing so rapidly, it has become difficult
even for the professionals to be sure of their ground in matters of
rail transit.

This study is intended to clarify some of the problems through a
discussion of the basic technological and economic characteristics

---

[7] Rail transit interests never tire of pointing out that a single
transit track can produce 40,000 passenger trips per hour, whereas
a single lane of highway uses just as much land to produce but 3,000
automobile passenger trips per hour. As will be discussed later in
this book, a transit track could produce as many trips as this per
hour (and more), but seldom does. On the basis of total trip production the disparity between rail transit and the automobile is never so great as those figures would suggest. Were highways to be
used intensively for bus transit, moreover, rail transit might
come off second best altogether in some situations.

In any case, the question of land use efficiency cannot be settled
merely on the basis of line-haul capacities. The argument over
them has therefore been more a hindrance than a help in putting rail
transit in sensible public perspective.

of rail transit systems. A description of the major physical components of these systems, their operational requirements, and their
costs forms the basis for this discussion. The study emphasizes
such characteristics as capacity and quality of service and attempts
to relate these to cost wherever possible. Finally, it attempts to
relate rail transit to the entire urban transportation scene of which
it is a part.

All of this discussion aims primarily at the urban planner and
transportation engineer, those professionals to whom transit capabilities are of definite concern, but whose knowledge of the subject
is too often restricted by a lack of technical literature. To this end,
we have included technical information which should enable the non-
technician to evaluate more intelligently the usual engineering re-
ports on rail transit schemes. No attempt has been made to present
this information in enough detail to make it of more than general interest to such specialists in the field as, say, transit car designers.
Our analysis of costs and operating characteristics is also not in the
detail required by the transit expert, although he may find we have
taken some different approaches to his problems. Beyond the professional readers we have also been mindful of the interested, but
professionally unconcerned, citizen who often plays a role in decisions on urban transportation problems.

This is a modest study. It makes no attempt, for instance, to de-
scribe future transit technology in detail. This stems partly from
the authors' lack of expertise in equipment technology and partly
from a conviction that the effect of technological innovation on over-
all system performance and costs will be only gradual in the years
immediately ahead. (We do discuss the subject of automation, because it deserves a less emotional treatment than the literature usually gives it.) We were also limited in our ability to employ refined
techniques of costing. It must be for the reader to judge whether
our cost results are thus too crude even for the general sort of picture we want to present.

Chapter 2

THE SUPPORTING WAY

The major physical components of a rail transit system are the
supporting way, the stations, the terminals, and the vehicles. In
rail systems the supporting way incorporates certain elements of
the vehicle guidance and power supply systems in addition to providing an obstacle-free surface upon which the vehicle is supported.
This chapter treats the characteristics of supporting ways and includes discussion of track and structures, power supply and distribution systems, and signal systems.[1] Cost data are presented at
the end of the chapter.

2.1 Supporting and Enclosing Structures

The general methods of supporting or enclosing present day rail
transit systems are well known. In areas where land is inexpensive
and readily available, the system can be supported on the ground in
the same way highways or railroads are supported. A forty-foot
strip of right of way is usually enough for a two-track line. At inter-
sections a surface system can be carried over the crossing traffic
by means of an elevated structure. When the crossings become too
frequent, it then becomes more economical to support the system
entirely on an elevated structure. In areas where land is very expensive or is not readily available for use, it may be more economical to support the system in an underground structure and thus avoid
disturbance of ground level activities altogether.

The configuration of supporting or enclosing structures depends on
other factors. For elevated structures, construction material and
number of tracks are the most important factors. A significant difference here is that, while the final shape of a subway is of little
concern, the final shape of an elevated structure may have a significant influence on neighboring land use.[2] In modern designs single

---

[1] The effect of signal systems on over-all capacity is treated
separately in Chapter 5.

[2] One should remember that most existing elevated structures are
relatively old, were built for heavyweight rolling stock, and are
therefore very massive. Present-day technology can provide elevated structures less bulky in nature and more pleasing in appearance. The modernistic appearance of monorail, for instance, would
be less dramatic if it were compared with the elevated structures
that could now be designed for conventional transit.

central column structures of steel, reinforced concrete, or prestressed concrete are often proposed. The use of prestressed
concrete is particularly advantageous, because it permits longer-
span structures and fewer columns, although this may also increase cost. If span lengths are held constant, the use of mass-
produced prefabricated elements can produce economies in concrete construction. Figure 2.1 shows a recently proposed design
for an elevated concrete structure.

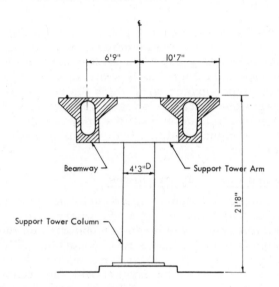

Figure 2.1. Typical supporting structure, elevated system.
Source: Daniel, Mann, Johnson, and Mendenhall, A Comparative Analysis of Rapid Transit System Equipment and Routes,
Report prepared for the Los Angeles Metropolitan Transit Authority, Los Angeles, August 26, 1960.

There is considerable variety in the configuration of subway systems and their methods of construction. The nature of the soil,
depth of construction, presence of utilities, and number of tracks
to be provided all affect the final form selected. All subway construction is, of course, costly. Because this cost is so often the
crucial factor in rail transit planning, it is worth discussing the
major alternatives in subway construction methods.
  Tunneling. This method involves the excavation of the subway
cross section with little or no disturbance of ground level activity
during the construction period. It is the most expensive method of
subway construction and is generally used only where no alternative exists. Tunneling is almost always restricted to deep subway
construction, that is, where the subway is located too far below the
ground surface to permit economical "cut-and-cover" construction.

In shallower facilities it may be used in sections where it is particularly undesirable to disturb the ground surface.

Tunnel construction is accomplished by the use of steel shields
and linings. At the leading end of the tunnel, the steel shield supports the peripheral earth and protects the workers. As excavation proceeds, the excavated section is supported with a permanent
steel lining. The shield is then pushed forward by jacking against
the previously erected lining. Excavated materials are removed
through work shafts to the ground surface, which may be placed at

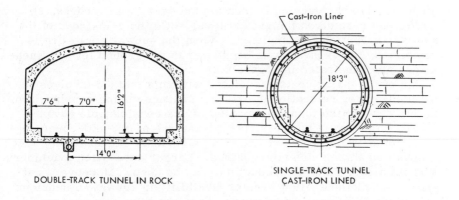

DOUBLE-TRACK TUNNEL IN ROCK

SINGLE-TRACK TUNNEL
CAST-IRON LINED

Figure 2.2. Typical cross sections of tunnels.
Source: Charles E. DeLeuw, Trans-Hudson Rapid Transit,
New York, 1957, Exhibits 17 and 19.

station locations. A permanent tunnel lining of concrete is placed
inside the steel lining.

Tunneling work is generally carried out under increased air
pressures. This places limitations on the number of hours a man
may work at any one time, thereby decreasing his work output.
This is one of the factors contributing to the higher cost of tunnel
construction. Costs are also increased, because the limit on maximum tunnel diameter (dictated by soil conditions and considerations of excavation volumes) usually requires constructing separate
tubes for each track. (Tunnels through rock may be an exception
in this respect.) Because of the small clearances much of the
available large-scale (and more economical) construction equipment cannot be used. The cost of future expansion is also higher
for tunnel sections than for other types discussed below.

Figure 2.2 shows sample tunnel cross sections.

Cut and Cover. As the name implies, this method involves the
excavation (cut) of earth from the ground surface to the level of
the subway floor, followed by backfilling (cover) from the subway
roof to the ground surface. In North America it has been the most
extensively used method of subway construction. Generally it is
much less expensive than tunneling. The major disadvantage of
this method lies in its disruption of ground level activities, including the demolition of any existing structures which stand on the
proposed subway route.

During construction the walls of the excavation are supported by
means of sheet piling driven down below the final depth of the subway. Preliminary excavation is carried out to a depth below any
utility conduits or pipes. These are temporarily suspended from
girders. Timber decking is then placed over these girders, so
traffic can resume on the ground level while the remainder of the
subway excavation is completed. When the subway enclosure is
completed, the excavation is backfilled to the ground level. These
stages are illustrated in Figure 2.3.

One of the major costs associated with this method involves the
maintenance or relocation of existing utilities during construction.
In this respect the tunneling method offers considerable advantages. In general, however, the advantages of cut-and-cover construction outweigh those of tunneling methods. For example, steel
linings and shields are not required. Larger excavation machinery,
with its higher rates of production, can be used. Moreover, cut-
and-cover methods allow greater flexibility in subway dimensions
and future additions. In any case, they are generally necessary
for station construction and for transition zones from surface or
elevated to subway facilities.

Figure 2.4 illustrates sample cut-and-cover cross sections.

ICANDA Method. A new Italian method of subway construction
known as the Milan Method has attracted attention recently. A
test section using this method has been constructed in Toronto under the direction of ICANDA engineers.[3] The major advantage of
this method is that it reduces the disturbance of normal city activities.

In this method trenches for the subway walls are excavated in
the appropriate location and to the required depth. As the excavation progresses, these trenches are filled with a slurry which
supports the sides. Steel reinforcing is then placed in the trenches
and the slurry is displaced by concrete. Up to this point street traffic continues. When the subway walls are completed, the street is
excavated to the depth of the subway roof. Concrete for the roof
is poured and the street is backfilled and reopened to traffic. This
leaves a subway structure consisting of two walls and a roof. The

---

[3] ICANDA Ltd. is the Canadian representative of the Italian firm
controlling the process.

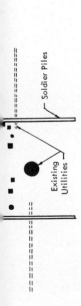

1. Soldier Piles are driven along outer limits of excavation.

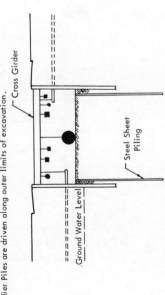

2. Excavation is completed below utilities. Transverse girders are placed across excavation. Utilities are temporarily suspended from girders. Sheet piling is driven from ground water level to bottom limits of excavation.

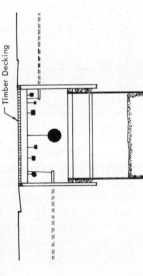

3. Timber decking is placed over girders for traffic. Subway excavation is completed.

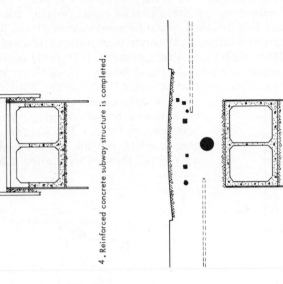

4. Reinforced concrete subway structure is completed.

5. Excavation is backfilled. Utilities are replaced and street pavement is reconstructed.

Figure 2.3. Stages of cut-and-cover construction.
Source: Charles E. DeLeuw, Downtown Rapid Transit Terminal Facilities for Cleveland, Chicago, 1959.

interior of the subway can be excavated and the floor poured without further disturbance to street traffic. The use of sheet piling and street decking is thus not required as in the cut-and-cover method.

Although the test section which was constructed in Toronto was more costly than cut-and-cover construction of equal length, there is reason to believe that this method could be cost competitive. The test section was constructed under soil conditions not particularly suitable for the ICANDA method and was too short (170 feet) to allow for efficient utilization of equipment and labor. In addition it was felt that certain improvements in design could be made for applications on this continent where utilities generally pose a larger problem than in Italy. The stages of construction for the ICANDA method are illustrated in Figure 2.5.

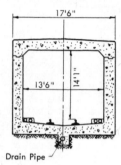

Single-Track Section

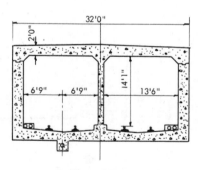

Double-Track Section

Figure 2.4. Typical cross sections of cut-and-cover subways.
Source: Charles E. De-leuw, Downtown Rapid Transit Terminal Facilities for Cleveland.

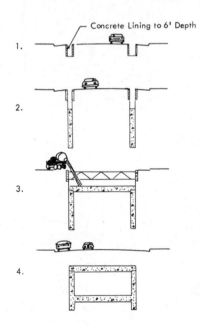

Figure 2.5. ICANDA method of subway construction.
After: Diagram from Toronto Transit Commission.

2.2 Track Structures

The track structure is an essential component of the supporting
way. Since it is thoroughly discussed in any text on railroad engineering, only a few remarks concerning this subject need be made
here. The track structure directly supports the weight of the rail
transit vehicle, guides its direction in the horizontal plane, and to
some extent limits vehicle speed. It is composed of three basic elements: rails, ties, and ballast. The condition of these elements
can have a significant effect on both costs of operation and passenger comfort.

Rails act as load spreaders and distribute the weight of the transit
vehicle among the ties. On this continent they are generally
spaced 4 feet $8\frac{1}{2}$ inches apart, the same gauge that is used on the
railroads. (This makes it possible to use transit vehicles on many
existing railroad facilities.) Recently, the use of welded rail
connections has improved the quality of ride that can be obtained
from steel-wheeled vehicles traveling on steel rails.

Ties act as load transmitters and transfer the distributed rail load
to the ballast. In this country they are almost always made of wood,
especially treated to resist deterioration. The replacement of ties
constitutes one of the major annual maintenance costs of the track
structure.

The ties are generally set in a bed of stone ballast. This ballast
section must in turn be heavy enough to resist side forces that tend
to slide the track laterally. The ballast must also be sufficiently
porous to permit proper drainage of the track structure. Ballast
sections are not usually provided in elevated systems since ties can
be anchored directly to the supporting structure. In subway systems
a modified form of ballast is now often used in which ties are completely eliminated. In this method the rails rest on tie plates supported on rubber pads. The pads in turn are embedded in a concrete
invert. Elimination of ties results in a height reduction of about 12
inches and also reduces annual maintenance costs.

Several recent transit proposals have suggested the use of rubber-
wheeled cars similar to those presently being used on an experimental line in Paris. Since these rubber wheels are not flanged, a
somewhat different track structure is required in order to provide
directional guidance for the vehicles. Proposed methods of incor-
porating such a guidance system into the average track structure
make use of horizontal wheels on the vehicles that bear against vertical guide rails. These guide rails would be located between the
running rails (which may be concrete or wood) or on the outboard
sides of the running rails. Guidance must also be provided during
the switching operation. This is accomplished by the use of conventional steel rails and wheels located on the inboard sides of the normal running rails and wheels. This is illustrated in Figure 2.6,
where both central and outboard guidance systems are shown.

2.3 Power Supply Systems

Urban rail transit systems generally employ electric power because it eliminates smoke, gases, and engine noise, and it is clean.

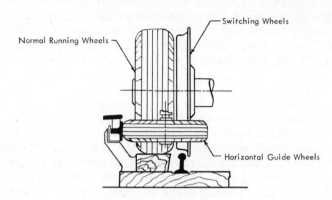

a) OUTBOARD GUIDANCE SYSTEM

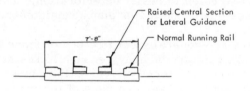

b) CENTRAL GUIDANCE SYSTEM

Figure 2.6.   Track details for rubber-wheeled vehicles. Sources: (a) Deleuw, Cather and Company, Mass Transportation Survey, National Capital Region, Chicago, 1959, Exhibit 10; (b) Daniel, Mann, Johnson, and Mendenhall, A Comparative Analysis of Rapid Transit System Equipment and Routes, p. 54.

For any reasonable level of operation, moreover, electric power is usually most economical. Although the initial costs of electrification are very high, its operating costs are very low. Systems utilizing individual power supplies on each train (such as diesel engines) are characterized by lower initial costs, but have much higher costs of operation.

Electrical power systems fall into two categories, alternating and direct current. These may in turn be subdivided into low and high voltage types. The number and size of power substations necessary to service a given line depend greatly on the voltage used. Power losses in an electrical system vary inversely as the square of the voltage for a given power requirement. Thus in a 600-volt system the losses will be 6.25 times greater than in a 1500-volt system.

For this reason power is usually generated for transmission at high voltage. Alternating current is most often used because the transmission of high voltage direct current involves a greater expense for line equipment.[4]

Low-voltage direct current is usually preferred in the vehicles themselves. Lower voltages minimize arcing or flashover between insulated elements, while the conversion of electrical energy to mechanical energy is more economical using d-c motors.[5] If this conversion of electrical power takes place on the transit vehicle itself, the necessary rectifier and transformer equipment adds substantially to the weight of the car. This in turn results in higher power costs at any given level of performance. Thus, in most systems power is transmitted to substations as high-voltage alternating current. There it is converted to low-voltage (600 volts is common) direct current by means of transformers and rectifiers. From the substations power reaches the vehicles through a distribution system which usually takes the form of an overhead wire or third rail. Generally the running rails of the track structure provide the return conductor.

Power substations are usually spaced at intervals of 1.5 to 2.5 miles. For long lines with a large number of power substations the problem of power supply becomes more involved, since power costs depend both on the quantity consumed and the number of different points at which it is necessary to deliver power. On one hand, power may be purchased at each substation at some specified rate. Alternatively, the transit company may choose to purchase power in larger quantities at only a few substations at some lower rate and then provide its own high voltage distribution system for the remaining substations. The best alternative depends upon the differences in annual power costs and in the annual cost of the distribution system.

2.4 Power Distribution Systems

The most common power distribution systems currently in use for rail transit are the pantograph and third-rail systems. Trolley pole transmission is still used for streetcar services and on a few rail transit lines which use streetcar-type equipment. Although the use of trolley poles does require a less costly overhead wire system, they are not generally proposed for new lines, because trolley poles can too easily jump off the wire (particularly during switching), and because trolley poles require manual operation. The remainder of the discussion will, therefore, be limited to pantograph and third-rail considerations.

----

[4] William W. Hay, Railroad Engineering (New York: John Wiley & Sons, 1953), p. 104.

[5] At low speeds, d-c motors produce high torque which is particularly important for rail transit operation where stops are frequent. These motors also exhibit a smoothness of control not found in a-c motors. See ibid., pp. 103-104.

Pantograph operation involves the use of an overhead wire and a collapsible-frame pickup located on the roof of the transit vehicle. The frame may be raised by air pressure or springs and is lowered by gravity. Carbon runners make contact between the pantograph and the trolley wire. These are of sufficient width to prevent loss of contact in the horizontal plane. Pantograph systems are generally used for high-voltage (low-amperage) power distribution where it is desirable to keep arcing distances as large as possible. An important advantage of this system is that the right of way need not be fenced off. A disadvantage is that under winter weather conditions the trolley wires may coat with ice and interrupt the power. In addition, considerable damage has occurred on some systems where refuse thrown from overpasses has landed on the pantograph and caused short circuits. For subway systems the most obvious disadvantage of a pantograph system is that it requires increased vertical clearance. This can increase over-all construction cost.

Third-rail distribution systems are the most widely used in rapid transit. Since the current-carrying capacity of the third rail is generally higher than that of the trolley wire, third rail is particularly adaptable to low-voltage systems. The rail itself is similar in shape to the running rails of the track and is usually made of high-conductivity steel. Contact between rail and vehicle is made by means of a contact shoe which may be of either the overrunning or underrunning types. Underrunning third rails are preferred in exposed areas where they provide better protection from snow and sleet. The disadvantages of third rail in elevated or open-cut facilities include the necessity of providing fencing and the possibility that the rail will be covered by snow. The proximity of the third rail to the ground involves greater hazard to workmen, although the likelihood of contact with personnel and foreign objects is reduced for the underrunning rail. In top-contact systems possible grounding resulting from an accumulation of wet snow may also occur because of the low clearances.

The initial installation costs for either third-rail or pantograph systems are approximately the same. Vehicle costs are slightly higher for pantograph operation. In addition, third-rail systems are considered to have longer lives and generally require less maintenance. These factors combined with clearance considerations for subway operation weigh heavily in favor of the use of third-rail distribution systems.

2.5 Signal Systems

The function of a rail transit signal system is to provide for the rapid movement of trains with minimum delay and maximum safety. Signal systems currently in operation make use of techniques in which a line is subdivided into a series of electrically insulated track sections known as blocks. Operations are based on   the principle that not more than one train may occupy a given block at any one time. The motorman of each train is informed of track occupancy in the blocks ahead through a system of electrically operated signals. In current practice, these may be of two types: wayside signals located at one side of the track, or cab signals located in the motorman's cab.[6] Newer methods of communication are being considered, however, in proposals for automated rail transit systems.

Wayside Signals. Early wayside signals were manually controlled by a man stationed at each signal. Today, practically all systems are automatic, making use of electrical track circuits for each block. These circuits are normally energized; when a train occupies a block, it shunts or short-circuits the energy to provide a block occupancy indication. Use of this active circuit, as opposed to a passive circuit in which the train would act as a circuit closer, has the advantage of providing a warning in the event of a broken rail or obstruction across the tracks. In addition, it is "fail-safe" in the event of a power failure.

Wayside signals generally display three aspects. A green signal indicates that the train may proceed at normal running speed. A yellow signal indicates that the next signal is red and that the train should proceed at reduced speed, prepared to stop at the next signal. A red signal indicates an imperative stop.

Most rapid transit signaling also includes automatic "train-stop" equipment. The train-stop is a mechanical device located next to the track which operates in conjunction with the signal. When a signal shows a stop indication, the train-stop is automatically raised. In the event a train attempts to pass the signal, this device trips a control on the lead car which applies the emergency brakes. Any train violating a red signal is thus automatically stopped, unless the motorman manually releases the train-stop in accordance with certain prescribed procedures.[7]

Wayside signals can also be used to control the speed of a train on curves or in the approaches to a station. With speed control signals, a timing apparatus is installed which clears each signal a predetermined number of seconds after the entrance of a train into its approach section. These time intervals are based on that portion of the deceleration curve (time versus speed) which should occur if the train is decelerating at the proper rate. If decelerating properly, the train will find that each successive signal clears before being reached; if decelerating too slowly, it will arrive before sufficient time has

---

[6] On this continent only wayside signals are currently in use for rapid transit operations. Several proposals for new transit lines have suggested the use of cab signals.

[7] These procedures generally include stopping at the signal, waiting a specified time, manually releasing the train-stop, and then proceeding at reduced speed.

elapsed for the next signal to clear. The automatic train-stop will then apply the brakes.

Speed-control wayside signals have two disadvantages from the standpoint of passenger comfort and safety. The ride tends to be similar in effect to the ride produced by an automobile driver traveling through a succession of traffic lights, slowing down or accelerating in anticipation of each light change, intent all the while not to stop. This is uncomfortable. More important, however, is the fact that a signal cannot distinguish between a train that is accelerating and one that is decelerating. For example, a train could enter a section below normal speed, accelerate and clear the next signal, but now at a higher speed than originally anticipated. Under these circumstances safe stopping protection might not be provided for the train ahead. In this respect, cab signals provide more positive speed control.

Cab Signals. Whereas a wayside signal conveys information to the motorman only as the train enters each block, cab signals provide continuous information throughout the block. Thus with wayside signaling, the motorman must abide by the indication last received and may not increase speed until such information is conveyed by the next signal. With cab signaling, on the other hand, the motorman can take advantage of a less restrictive indication as soon as the track ahead warrants it and need not wait until he reaches the next block signal.

Cab signals are also controlled by an electrical track circuit. This circuit makes use of an alternating current in the rails of each block which is uniformly interrupted at a rate indicating the condition of the track ahead. This interruption rate, or code rate, determines the aspect displayed by the cab signal and governs the maximum speed of the train.

Each signal indicates a maximum allowable speed which is in effect so long as that signal is displayed. Several measures are employed to enforce compliance with the speed restriction. At maximum speed a separate warning light is displayed in the cab; at 1 mile per hour above the maximum speed, a warning bell rings; at 2 miles per hour above maximum speed, the train is automatically brought to a stop. Moreover, upon receiving an indication to reduce speed, the motorman must initiate service braking within a prescribed time to prevent automatic application of emergency brakes. In addition, an indication to proceed at the lowest permissible speed must always be acknowledged by the motorman regardless of the train speed at the time to prevent automatic stopping.

Automated Signals. The development of automated transit systems depends in part on changes in the theory behind rail transit signaling. Both wayside and cab signaling methods are based on the principle of maintaining a safe distance between successive trains, commensurate with train speed. In both these systems, the following train is concerned with the location of the preceding train. In completely

automated systems, on the other hand, the following train would
be concerned with the operating condition of the preceding train
—whether stopped, accelerating, decelerating, or traveling at a
constant speed. Since the preceding train would not stop instan-
taneously, the distance between trains would have to be only such
as to allow the following train sufficient time to initiate the proper action. As the means of communication between trains was
improved, this distance between trains could be reduced corre-
spondingly.[8]

Several methods of automatic signaling and train control have
been suggested recently for both proposed and existing rail transit
facilities.[9] The differences between these methods depend in part
upon the type of operation to be automated. In shuttle services
where there are only two terminals and no intermediate stations,
and where only one train is concerned, the problem is not unlike
that of an automatic elevator. In the case of mainline operation,
the presence of more than one train on the same track and the possibility of vehicle collisions make the problem more difficult.

In general, methods of automation currently under consideration
employ the use of a control center which maintains a continuous
record of the location and speed of all trains in the system.   By
means of high-speed computers, train performance can be compared with a master schedule, and, where necessary, corrective
instructions can be relayed to the trains. The speed and location
of pairs of trains can be observed by the use of auxiliary components, and the proper relationship between leading and following
trains of every pair can be maintained through the communication
system. The basic advantage of these methods is their ability to
adapt quickly to changing conditions.

2.6 Aesthetic and Noise Considerations

At the beginning of this chapter some remarks were made concerning the effect of subway, elevated, and at-level transit facilities on
surrounding land use. Since any discussion of the relative aesthetic
values of these three types of facilities must by necessity be sub-
jective in nature, the further discussion here will be brief as well.

It has already been pointed out that the final structural configuration of subway facilities is of little concern to the nonriding public
since it is out of sight. If one believes that all transportation

---

[8]This is discussed in more detail in Appendix A.

[9]See for example, Daniel, Mann, Johnson, and Mendenhall, A
Comparative Analysis of Rapid Transit System Equipment and
Routes, Report prepared for the Los Angeles Metropolitan Transit Authority, Los Angeles, August 26, 1960, pp. 45-47, or General Electric Company, San Francisco Bay Area Rapid Transit
District Automatic Train Control System, February 5, 1960, 13
pp. mimeographed.

facilities must necessarily detract from the aesthetic values of
the city form, then subway facilities are the least offensive (and
therefore most desirable) of the three basic possibilities. From
the point of view of the passengers, however, subways are probably the least pleasant facility—except for those who enjoy the apparent high speeds produced by the proximity of the subway walls.
In subway proposals, therefore, consideration should be given to
questions of how subways can be made more pleasant for their
riders.

Wherever elevated transportation facilities of any type have been
placed over city streets, the adjacent areas tend to be blighted.
The restriction of light and air under elevated transit structures
and in adjacent buildings, coupled with increased noise levels, has
usually resulted in decreased desirability of the adjacent land for
business or residential purposes. In many cases, even though the
elevated structures have been constructed in order to allow streets
to be used for other purposes, the street space under these facilities has still been inefficiently utilized.

The displeasing appearance of elevated structures can be attributed partly to their age and the fact that available materials and
the use of heavyweight rolling stock demanded massive structural
shapes. There is little doubt that elevated structures could be designed and constructed today which would be much smaller in size
and more pleasing in appearance, but which would at the same time
provide comparable capacity. Under the proper circumstances,
elevated facilities are not entirely undesirable. They need not be
placed over road rights of way. Separate, and thus narrower,
rights of way may be used for each track or the entire structure
may be placed higher up in order to reduce light and air losses.
There will be cases where streets are sufficiently wide to accept
elevated structures without significant loss of light and air. Where
central malls are available, the structure may not in any way reduce the amount of street space available for other purposes.
From the aesthetic point of view, well-designed and properly located elevated structures may even add to the visual character of
the surroundings. Moreover, elevated facilities are generally
much more pleasant for the passengers than subways. This is
particularly true when the location of these facilities provides a
good view of the city.

The relative noise levels produced by various types of rail transit
facilities are also important.[10] Noise arises from transit vehicles
as a result of interactions between wheels and the roadway surface

---

[10] The following discussion is based largely on a study made for
the proposed Los Angeles Rapid Transit System. See Bolt Beranek and Newman Inc., Considerations of Noise Control for the
Proposed Los Angeles Mass Rapid Transit System, Report No.
712, Los Angeles, 1960.

and because of aerodynamic turbulence around the wheels and under the vehicle. The level of this noise depends on many factors
such as irregularities in track surface, eccentricity of wheels,
the nature of the track joint, and the relative degree of damping
which can be effected. Damping of noise vibrations may be accomplished in steel wheels by providing a rubber or other vibration
absorption element between wheel rim and hub, though this type of
wheel has generally proved unacceptable for other reasons. Noise
vibrations may also be damped by embedding rails in pavement or
supporting them on some absorbent material. The noise level may
also be reduced significantly by the use of welded instead of bolted
rail connections. The use of sound-absorbent shielding materials
has also been suggested, but this method may be undesirable aesthetically.

The degree to which noise level becomes important depends upon
the nature of the other activities in the area, the distance from the
noise source to these activities, and the relation between the existing background noise and the noise level produced by the transit facility. In addition to the actual measurable noise level (in decibels),
the quality and character of the noise is also a consideration: High-
frequency noises sound louder than low-frequency noises of the
same intensity.

In order to account for noise intensity, as well as for differences
in noise quality, the Los Angeles study makes use of a Perceived
Noise Level measure.[11] In evaluating the effect of transit facility
noise, this measure can compare the noise level produced by the
transit facility itself with existing background noise levels. The
general character of the noise produced by steel-wheeled and rubber-tired vehicles may also be of some importance. In general the
public is familiar with the noise produced by rubber tires operating
on paved surfaces. In cases where perceived noise levels might
be equivalent for both steel and rubber-wheeled vehicles, the noise
from the steel wheels may therefore be more noticeably objectionable. (The effect of noise produced inside the transit vehicles is
also a consideration. This is discussed in Chapter 4.)

2.7 Costs of Construction

So many factors can affect the construction costs of rail transit
facilities, that differences in costs, even for facilities that to the
eye are identical, may be as large in magnitude as the estimates
themselves. Such variations in cost are not really surprising when
some of the major factors are examined.

The cost of a rail transit facility may be significantly affected by
the cost of acquiring right of way. Facilities that can be constructed
without the necessity of taking land already in use will cost

---

[11] Ibid., p. 22.

considerably less than identical facilities requiring the demolition
of existing structures. Sections of open-cut rail transit track that
were constructed in Cleveland on an existing railroad right of way,
for instance, cost much less than a similar section in Toronto
where it was necessary to acquire private lands in built-up areas.

The cost of temporary maintenance or relocation of previously
existing underground utilities can be a significant part of total cut-
and-cover subway construction costs. A variation in the amount
of these existing utilities will therefore affect costs. The nature
of adjacent buildings and structures may also have a significant effect on subway construction costs. Where subways are located under narrow streets or where buildings are large, underpinning of
adjacent structures may be required. This can involve large costs.

The total length of a rail line may also affect the costs of construction on a route-mile basis. In the case of a simple two-track
line with crossovers at each end, the cost per mile will decrease
as the total line length increases, since the cost of the crossover
signal system will be distributed over a longer length. Similarly,
in the case of driven tunnels the cost of the tunnel shields will be
less per route-mile as the line length increases. These are simply examples of "spreading the overhead" over a longer line.

There are still other factors affecting construction costs. Topog-
raphy will be important; the costs for similar facilities will be different for hilly terrain than for flat areas. Geological and hydro-
logical conditions can be even more important. Finally, the cost
of labor and materials can be crucial.

Because construction costs do depend upon so many factors, it
is difficult to generalize about them, and average costs are not very
reliable. With this in mind, some representative cost figures have
been presented in Table 2.1 for various types of rail transit facilities.
These costs were assembled primarily from estimates for proposed
facilities and from cost experiences on facilities constructed during
the past six years. Most of the available data concern cut-and-cover
subway costs, and for this reason a range can be shown for these
costs. The figures here include the costs of

> Track and Structures
> Relocation and Maintenance of Utilities
> Power Supply and Distribution Systems
> Transmission Systems
> Signal Systems

Station costs and the cost of rolling stock are discussed in the following chapters. They are not included here. Right-of-way costs,
for reasons already mentioned, cannot be generalized to any degree
and are therefore not included. These figures also do not include
the costs of engineering (generally 10 per cent) and contingencies
(generally 15 per cent) that are customarily added to the total costs.

Table 2.1. Costs of Construction for Various Types of Two-
Track Rail Transit Facilities (1959-1960 prices)

Type of Facility	Average Cost per Route-Mile (In $1,000)
Cut and Cover	14,000 (Range 9,900-17,800)
Tunnel	15,300
Elevated	3,200
Open Cut	2,600
At Level*	2,100

*This particular figure was obtained for construction of a segment
of Chicago's Congress Street Line. Mr. E. L. Tennyson, Transit
Operations Engineer for the City of Philadelphia, stated in a letter
to R. M. Soberman dated July 10, 1961: "The finished tracks themselves should not cost more than $300,000 . . . and power supply
$500,000 for heavy traffic. With lighter traffic, the power supply
cost would drop." Thus costs might conceivably drop to $800,000
per double-track-mile for this type of construction.

Chapter 3

STATIONS

Social acceptability and a pleasing physical appearance have already been mentioned as important factors in the evaluation of rail transit systems. These noneconomic factors are of significance to both users and nonusers alike. The characteristics of the supporting way affect the nonusers primarily, while those of the vehicle have the greatest effect on users. The appearance of stations and terminals affect both groups: nonusers are forced to live with the appearance of the station structure and the high level of activity focused around it, while users spend time there in transferring from one mode of transportation to another.

Stations also play an important role in the economics of transit systems. The design and layout of the stations affect the time necessary for trains to load and unload. This may in turn affect line capacity and equipment utilization. (This is discussed in Chapter 5.) Station arrangement can also have a significant effect on costs of operation with respect to fare collection and transfer facilities. This may, in fact, be the area of operations where some of the greatest gains in reducing present costs can be made.

The alternatives in station layout are, of course, innumerable. As with many other aspects of rail transit facilities, there is no single solution that will be optimum in every case. This is particularly true where it is necessary to provide interchange facilities at stations located at the junction of more than one line or type of service. Some aspects of station design, however, are subject to generalizations of a qualitative if not quantitative nature, and these are discussed in the remainder of this chapter.

3.1 Station Arrangement

Stations are collectors and distributors. They accommodate large concentrations of transit riders at various points along the route. This concentration should be accomplished with a minimum of confusion, annoyance, and effort for passengers, and with a maximum of efficiency for train loading and unloading operations. Ideally the station layout should be such that passengers find themselves located along the platform in uniform groups at each transit car doorway. While this is not literally possible, it is an important factor in selecting the locations of stairways, turnstiles, escalators, and passageways.[1]

Basically stations are of either the central or side platform type. Figures 3.1 to 3.3 show several examples of these. Central platforms have the advantage of requiring a minimum of duplication of facilities. At best the requirements for turnstiles, ticket boxes, and escalators are one-half those of side platforms while at worst they are equal. Total platform width will generally be less for central platforms since the same platform can be used to accommodate both the morning and evening peaks. In the case of side platforms each platform will have to be of sufficient width to accommodate peak traffic. Central platforms, however, will generally require a more extensive system of passageways and stairways to cross passengers over or under street traffic. Side platforms are more adaptable to direct access from sidewalks.

The relative advantages and disadvantages of each arrangement must be weighed against differences in cost in order to determine the best solution. In general, it would seem that the central platform arrangement is preferable for less heavily used stations where one cashier and escalator are sufficient to handle the traffic. Side platform arrangements are probably preferable for heavy traffic points. This arrangement also provides greater flexibility, in that a two-track system may be expanded to four tracks without the construction of additional platforms or station facilities. In the case of central platform arrangements it would be necessary to provide two additional platforms. Since in general land values will rise in the area adjacent to new station facilities, the cost of widening the station to provide these additional platform facilities could be prohibitive.

Both central and side platform stations may be constructed using single- or multiple-level arrangements. In the single-level station, ticketing, fare collection, and loading operations take place at the same level. In two-level stations a mezzanine is provided for ticketing and fare collection facilities while a separate level is provided for train loading and unloading. This can be particularly desirable for heavily used stations. A mezzanine arrangement for side platform stations permits ticketing and fare collection facilities to be shared, thereby obviating the necessity of providing these facilities on each platform. The use of two-level stations in subways may not always be possible, however, depending upon the depth at which the track is located.

Two-level stations also offer a means of controlling the number of passengers waiting on the platform at any one time. By using the mezzanine as a holding zone whenever the number of passengers on the platform becomes too large, scheduled train loading times

---

[1] Unless otherwise noted, the remarks in this chapter refer to two-track facilities.

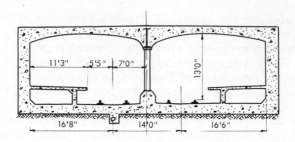

Station Structure – Cut and Cover

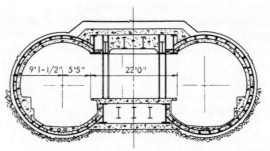

Station Structure – Cast Iron Lined

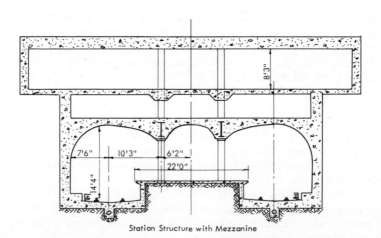

Station Structure with Mezzanine

Figure 3.1.   Typical subway station sections.
Source: Charles E. DeLeuw, Trans-Hudson Rapid Transit,
New York, 1957.

may be maintained. Such a procedure, however, can meet with
serious objections from the public unless carried out in conjunction with an adequate public information program.

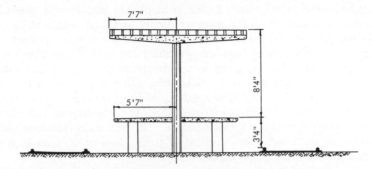

Figure 3.2. Typical surface station section.
Source: Cleveland Transit System, Rapid Transit Extension
to Cleveland Hopkins Airport, Cleveland, 1960.

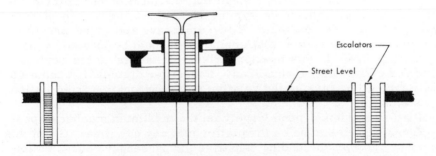

Figure 3.3. Proposed elevated station section.
Source: Daniel, Mann, Johnson, and Mendenhall, A Comparative Analysis of Rapid Transit Equipment and Routes, Report
prepared for the Los Angeles Metropolitan Transit Authority,
Los Angeles, August 26, 1960.

3.2 Platform and Passageway Capacities

Platforms. The arrangement of entrances and exits with respect to station platforms can have a considerable effect on the
time required to load and unload trains. For a given train length
and number of passengers to be loaded, loading time will depend
upon the distribution of passengers along the platform, the ratio
of total door length to car length (see Section 4.5), and the relative

size of movements into and out of the train.[2]   Loading time is some
function of the maximum number of passengers using any one train
door, and this number is minimized when the number of passengers using each door is equal.   Obtaining a uniform distribution of
passengers along the platform is difficult.   Passengers tend to lo-
cate themselves along the platform at points which will provide
them with a favorable exit upon arriving at their destination, or at
points which they feel will be less crowded than other points.   During rush hours there is less opportunity for this redistribution to
take place, since passengers are usually more concerned with the
problem of boarding the train than with their location on it.   Thus,
provisions made for uniform loading of long trains in peak hours
may not result in the most efficient loading conditions for shorter
trains operated in the nonrush hours.   In this case loading time is
usually less than the scheduled stop time, however, and is therefore not a major consideration.

The location of platform entrances also affects the relative loading of each car in the train.   If entry to the platform is at its center,
the number of passengers in the end cars tends to be less than that
of the center cars.   Similarly, passenger loadings in the central
cars tend to fall off if there is access to the platform only at the
ends.   These considerations mean that the location of platform entry points ideally should be symmetrical about the center of the
longest train.   For example, if two stairways are to be provided
for access to the station platform, they should be located at the
quarter points.   In this manner walking distances to the central
and end cars would be equalized.   Passenger distribution can also
be improved by varying the relative entrance location from station
to station.

Platform widths depend largely on the maximum number of passengers expected to be on the platform at any one time.   Given this
number, acceptable loading densities (or passenger concentration
in terms of passengers per square foot of platform) can be applied
to determine the required platform width.   Very little information
is available, however, upon which the determination of an appropriate loading density can be based.   Factors influencing this density include the nature of various movements that will take place
on the platform and the average distances passengers will walk
from their points of entry to the locations at which they will board
the train.   Lower concentrations than those used in the transit cars
themselves (0.2-0.5 passenger per square foot) are necessary if entering and leaving passengers are to pass one another freely.   When
adequate widths are not provided, passengers leaving the train are

[2] Platforms could conceivably be used which were shorter than
trains if cars were loaded through end doors.   From the standpoint of both loading time and safety, however, this is not a particularly desirable arrangement for rapid transit operations.

prevented from doing so rapidly, with the result that station stop times are greatly increased and line capacity reduced. The selection of appropriate platform widths, then, is not a problem to be passed over lightly. In the absence of sufficient analytical data, the selection of an appropriate loading density and platform width requires considerable judgment. Currently proposed widths for side platforms range from 8 feet for low-density stations to 12 feet for high-density stations. For central platforms, widths range from 15 to 30 feet.

Passageways. The term "passageways" refers to all means of access to and from station platforms and includes corridors, stairways, and escalators. The figures used in this discussion are those obtained from experiments conducted for the preliminary planning of a new subway in London.[3]

In determining the desirable capacity and arrangement of passageways, three rather simple rules must be kept in mind. The first of these states that passageway capacity to a platform should not be greater than the number of people that can be carried away by the trains. If passenger backup is unavoidable during certain periods, then the platform is not the place for this backup to occur if scheduled stop times are to be maintained. Second, the number of conflicts between different distinct passenger flows should be minimized. Third, long passageways between facilities should be avoided. This is always one of the major complaints made about interchange facilities.

Table 3.1. Passageway Capacities

Type of Passageway (Widths over 4 feet)	Design Flow in Passengers per Foot of Width per Minute	
	London	Paris
Level Corridor	27	30.5
Upward Stairs	19	18.3
Downward Stairs	21	22.8

The London experiments shows that the capacity of corridors and stairs vary in proportion to corridor width for widths greater than 4 feet. In addition, the walking speed of passengers tends to decrease as the concentration (crowding) of passengers increases. Maximum capacity for any given corridor width occurs at a concentration of about 0.4 person per square foot. At this concentration, however, walking speeds are reduced to a "shuffle," which is not a particularly desirable situation. These tests have also shown that to prevent staircases from becoming bottlenecks they

[3]Frank Turner, "Preliminary Planning for a New Tube Railway Across London," Proceedings of the Institution of Civil Engineers, Vol. 12, January 1959.

must be widened by approximately 50 per cent of the corridor width.
Flow figures for the Paris Métro are in good agreement with the London figures. Table 3.1 illustrates the findings of studies in both cities.

3.3 Fare Collection

Fare collection methods depend principally upon whether a single
fare or zone fare structure is used for the system. Most rail
transit properties on this continent currently make use of single-fare
systems; that is, only one fare is charged regardless of trip length.
Many European systems use zone fares where the charge is propor-
tionate to the distance traveled.[4]

Single-Fare Systems. Single-fare systems are the simplest to
operate, since the fare must be collected only once. The standard
method of fare collection in single-fare systems involves the use
of turnstiles. In general, turnstiles will accept either transit to-
kens or the correct change, although in some cases separate turnstiles operated by a cashier are provided for cash fares. Cashier-
operated turnstiles are also used where special fares or transfers
are used. Transfer-issuing machines are usually provided as separate units or may be incorporated in the turnstile. Entrance turnstiles are often used in the reverse direction to provide exit facilities in addition to specially provided exit turnstiles or baffle gates.
A recent trend in some properties has been to have fares collected
on the trains during certain hours of the day. In this case some
provision must be made for the free operation of turnstiles that are
normally operated by fares. Table 3.2 gives figures indicative of
the practical capacities of standard turnstiles.

Zone-Fare Systems. There is little doubt that for long transit
lines a zone-fare system based upon the distance traveled is both
equitable and desirable. Proposals have also been made for the
use of a fare structure based on the time of day during which the
trip takes place.[5] This idea has merit, because the cost of carrying a passenger during rush hours is much higher than during off-
peak hours. This concept is applied in other forms of transport.

----

[4] There are some examples of zone-fare systems in the United
States such as Chicago's Howard Street-Evanston Line, Cleveland's Shaker Heights Line, and the conversion in October 1961,
of Boston's Highland Branch to a zone-fare system. By and large,
however, these are examples of zone fares collected on the train
by conductors or motormen. Only with a relatively small number
of zones will this be operationally efficient. On the London system a more flexible zone-fare system can be used, because fares
are collected in the stations.
[5] William S. Vickery, The Revision of the Rapid Transit Fare
Structure of the City of New York, Mayor's Committee on Man-
agement Survey of the City of New York, Technical Monograph
3, New York, 1952.

Table 3.2. Practical Operating Capacity of Standard Turnstiles*

Type of Turnstile	Capacity in Persons per Minute
Free or Cashier Operated:	
Free Admission	60
With Ticket Collector	25-35
With Cash Transaction	20-35
Coin-Operated:	
Single Fare	50
Multiple Fare	40
Baffle Gate:	
Nonregistering Exit	40-45
Coin-Operated	20-35

*Institute of Traffic Engineers, Traffic Engineering Handbook, New Haven, 1950, p. 101.

Lower fares are charged for midweek travel by air, for instance. (Notice also that automobile operating costs are less during the nonrush hours.) An increase in demand during the rush hours generally requires an increase in capacity, whereas the same increase in demand during the nonrush hours results in more efficient utilization of existing capacity.

With zone- or time-based fare systems, however, the mechanics of fare collection constitute a major problem. In both "pay as you leave" or "pay as you enter" systems the passenger must be issued some means of identification upon entering the system to indicate (in the first case) the fare that must be paid at the destination or (in the second case) the fare that has already been paid. In a poorly designed system the added cost of collecting this identification and the variable fare may be as much as or more than the increase in revenues. The problem is to design a system of zone fares, the collection cost of which is independent or almost independent of the number of passengers handled. Such a system would probably involve some degree of automation.

Several methods of semiautomatic zone-fare collection systems have been suggested for both proposed and existing rail transit facilities. Basically these methods involve the following operations. A token or ticket purchased at the origin station is retained by the passenger until arrival at his destination. The purchase price of the token is determined from a fare schedule which is based on the length of trip and which may or may not take into account day of the week and time of the day. When the passenger arrives at his destination, the token is checked by electromechanical means to ensure that the proper fare has been paid. Up to this point the sequence is automatic, inasmuch as various auxiliary change-

making machines can be provided for purchase of the fare. If the
fare is correct, the passenger can pass through the exit turnstile.
If the proper fare has not been paid, an attendant is summoned to
collect the difference. Several modifications of this system have
been suggested. For example, the purchase price at the origin
may be the same for every destination, and a refund obtained at
the destination. Basically these systems are the same, however;
all require that each trip be paid for separately at the time the
trip is made. This is obviously inconvenient for the daily users.

The flexibility of the previous system might be improved by two
modifications. Convenience for daily users or commuters could
be increased by the use of passes that would be valid for a certain
length of time or a certain number of trips. The pass would be
identified with code numbers so that it could be used only for certain stations. For travel outside these limits, access or exit
could be gained only if the appropriate additional fare were paid.
Here again, electromechanical devices could be employed to read
the passes and indicate the additional fare required. This is basically the same system as is used in the London Underground, but
with the substitution of automatic readers for human ticket checkers.

A somewhat more elaborate system that has been suggested em-
ploys the use of credit cards which would be inserted in an automatic reader at the origin and destination of each trip. Each reader would record the credit card number, station, and time of trip.
By means of electronic data-processing techniques, trip origins
and destinations could be matched, fares assessed, and bills
mailed out periodically. This method appears technically feasible
and has considerable merit. For each particular system, detailed
costs analyses would be necessary, however, in order to determine
its economic feasibility. Certain minimum fare-collection facilities would be necessary in any case for passengers not carrying
credit cards.

3.4 Turnaround Facilities

At terminal stations provision must be made for turning trains
around, that is, transferring them to the opposite track of a two-
track system. Three general methods of accomplishing this are
in use.

The simplest method of turning trains around is to provide a
loop for this purpose beyond the last station on the line. No switching is necessary during the operation, and signaling problems are
relatively simple. In addition, it is not necessary for the motorman to move to the opposite end of the train. On the other hand,
turnaround loops require substantial land area and cannot always
be provided in built-up urban areas.

A more common method of turning trains around makes use of
a system in which main-line tracks extend beyond the terminal

station, spreading out and multiplying to form a fanlike arrangement. Each main track has access to all the spokes of the fan. A
train may be turned around by running forward from the main track
onto one of the spokes and then "backing" on to the other track. The
spokes of the "fan" also serve as storage space for extra cars during off-peak hours and trains can be broken down easily by "back-
ing-off" only the desired number of cars. Under this system, however, it is necessary for the motorman to change ends at some
point in the switching process.

A third turnaround method makes use of a track "crossover" located in the approach to the station. A train approaching the terminal station either remains on the same track or crosses over to
the opposite track depending upon which of the two tracks is occupied by a train already in the station. If the approaching train does
cross over, it will then be on the proper track for the return trip
after unloading and loading passengers. Otherwise, the crossover
operation takes place after the train has left the station on the return trip. Special signaling provisions must be made to ensure that
only one train attempts to use the crossover at a time. The crossover method has the advantage, however, of not requiring additional land for the turnaround operation beyond the terminal station.

3.5 Station Costs

The preceding chapter discussed some of the factors that can
cause wide variation in the construction costs of supporting ways.
These same factors affect station costs. Differences in general
station layout and arrangement are additional factors to be considered.

Table 3.3. Rail Transit Station Finish Costs (Over and above
basic track and structures cost—1959-1960 prices)

Station Type	Cost Range (In 1000's)
Cut and Cover	420-2400
Elevated	480-720
Open Cut	400-600
Median Strip	160-480

Note: Escalators will add another
$30,000 to $40,000 each.

Table 3.3 gives representative ranges of cost for various types
of stations able to accommodate trains up to 600 feet in length.
These costs are generally referred to as "station finish" costs,
since they do not include the cost of providing the track and
structures contained within the station limits. Cost ranges are

given instead of average costs, as stations which are physically
similar will usually differ with respect to the quantity and type of
equipment they contain (as for example, escalators, the cost of
which is also shown) or with respect to their means of access. The
particularly wide range of costs for subway stations depends
largely on whether single-level or multilevel arrangements are
used.[6]

_____

[6] Note that the total costs of multilevel stations will be higher
because of the greater amount of excavation and the greater
depth at which it takes place.

Chapter 4

RAIL TRANSIT VEHICLES

The vehicles of a rail transit system play a crucial role in its
over-all success. Vehicle "performance" (capability for acceleration, deceleration, and high running speeds) is a principal determinant of a system's ability to offer competitive over-all trip
times. Vehicle appearance and interior arrangement are principal determinants of a system's aesthetic acceptability and of passenger comfort. Vehicle design affects operating and, in particular, electric power costs, as well as maintenance costs.

It is no accident, then, that transit planning studies often em-
phasize vehicle configuration and design details. Similarly, it is
appropriate that we devote considerable attention to rail transit
vehicles here.

4.1 Vehicle Components

Structure. Structurally a rail transit car may be thought of as
a girder or beam simply supported near each end by the vehicle
trucks. The roof and floor provide the strength to resist bending
moment stresses and are analogous to the beam flanges. The
sides, generally reinforced by side sills, act as the beam web
and provide the necessary shear strength. (This shear strength
is critical at the door openings, where the least amount of side
material is available.) In general, the beam strength that a car
requires to carry the vertical load provides a compressive
strength which is more than adequate to carry normal end loadings. Car body and equipment weight usually comprises approximately 50 per cent of total vehicle weight.

Trucks. The vehicle truck is essentially a load distributing device which transmits the vertical load of the car through a series
of bearings, springs, and wheels to the track structure, as shown
in Figure 4.1. It also houses the drive system of the vehicle. In
some designs the weight of the car is received by a central bearing plate located on the truck bolster, which in turn is supported
by combinations of coil and, in some cases, air springs. The
springs then transmit the load through side frames to the wheels
and ultimately to the track. In other designs the car weight is
carried directly by the side frames through side-bearing plates,
the springs being located between the car body and the bolster.
Where both coil springs and air springs are used, the former

37

generally support the empty weight of the car body while the latter maintain constant floor heights under varying live load.

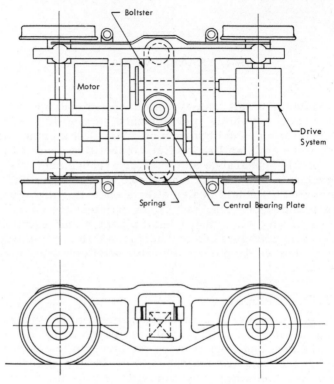

Figure 4.1. Typical truck design.
Source: Chicago Transit Authority.

Truck weights themselves have averaged approximately 20,000 pounds each, but drop as low as 11,000 pounds for some of the newer equipment now in use. Chicago has tested experimental cars with 9,000-pound trucks.

Traction Motors and Controls. Traction motors can be mounted directly on each axle of a truck. On most postwar equipment, however, traction motors are frame-mounted on a spring-supported member and drive the axles by means of flexible coupling connections. Motor speed can be variously controlled by connecting resistances in series with the motors, by alternating between series and parallel operation of the motors, or by varying motor field strength.[1] These electrical controls may be combined with the braking controls in the form of a single master controller by

---

[1] Reasons for the use of low-voltage direct-current motors in rail transit vehicles were given in Chapter 2.

means of which the operator can either accelerate or decelerate the train.

4.2 Weight Considerations

Weight is one of the most important single considerations in vehicle design. Vehicles presently in use range in weight from 900 to 1400 pounds per foot of length. Vehicles weighing 750 pounds per foot are in the design stage. This variation is not due to age differentials alone. New equipment can be found in both light and heavy weight categories. As is discussed below, there is no clear-cut current opinion about what the ideal weight should be.

There is a definite trend, however, toward the continued development of lightweight rail transit equipment, both by companies well-established in the field and by new manufacturers. In general, the advantages and disadvantages of lighter-weight equipment can be examined under the following headings:

1. Safety (resistance to buckling in the event of collision).
2. Power requirements (for a given level of performance).
3. Maintenance costs (of both equipment and track).
4. Riding qualities.
5. Vehicle life.

Safety. In theory, there should be no collisions in properly signalized rail transit systems. In actual practice, rear-end collisions do occur. For this reason, the resistance to buckling or buffing strength of transit cars is important. One of the reasons advanced for the continued use of heavyweight equipment is that it generally has a higher buffing strength. On the other hand it may be argued that the heavier weight equipment requires a greater dissipation of energy should a collision occur, with the net result that no improvement in safety is achieved.

The argument might be resolved by comparing the relationship between buffing strength and energy dissipation as a function of weight. Buffing strength, however, may not be the sole criterion for evaluating the safety of cars in the event of collision. It might conceivably be safer to have the car buckle at the ends, thus absorbing some of the kinetic energy which must be dissipated, than to have the car remain rigid while the passengers absorb the decelerating force by being thrown against the bulkheads. Where cars are very heavily loaded, however, no amount of end buckling would be permissible. None of these questions has been resolved to the satisfaction of all equipment designers in the industry.

Power Requirements. Basic laws of physics dictate that the power required to accelerate a vehicle or to propel it at constant speed is a direct function of the weight of the vehicle. If transit car designs are equal in every respect except weight, an additional expenditure for the lighter vehicle may be economically justified by its lower annual power costs. The amount of this additional expenditure is equal to the capitalized value of the annual savings in operating costs computed over the life of the vehicle. For the power cost data of Table 6.4, this amount would range from $800 to $2400 per ton of weight saved (assuming an interest rate of 5 per cent, a car life of 35 years, and an annual car mileage of 40,000).

Maintenance Costs. Many proponents of heavyweight transit vehicles argue that maintenance costs over the life of the vehicle are considerably lower for heavy equipment than for light. The equipment maintenance figures obtained from various transit operating properties do not substantiate this claim—but they do not refute it, either. The difficulty is that observed variations in maintenance costs may be attributed to many factors other than weight differential. In the first place, the lightweight equipment in use is generally newer than the heavyweight equipment, and for this reason requires less maintenance. Second, different properties have different ideas about maintenance and different requirements for maintenance. A property which washes its cars daily and paints frequently will (other things being equal) have higher maintenance costs than one which does not; one property may have higher repair costs due to vandalism than another. An adequate answer to the relationship between car weight and equipment maintenance costs would, therefore, require a careful comparison of the operation of both light and heavy equipment on the same property over a long period of time. A good comparison of this sort is not yet available.

The effect of vehicle weight on track maintenance costs is more easily determined, since they generally vary directly with tonnage and, hence, car weight passing over the track. Chapter 6 will discuss this further.

Riding Qualities. The effect of car weight on riding qualities is another highly speculative problem. Riding quality is primarily a function of the condition of the track and the characteristics of the truck suspension system. The extent to which it also depends upon vehicle weight has never been clear.

The experience of one of the authors is that the quality of ride experienced in lightweight equipment at high speed[2] was not significantly different from that experienced in heavy equipment at lower speed.[3] At the vehicle speeds presently contemplated for some new transit facilities,[4] however, the effect of car weight on riding quality may be more significant.

---

[2] A 44,000-pound car traveling at 40-45 miles per hour in Chicago's Congress Street Line.

[3] An 83,000-pound car traveling at 20 miles per hour in the Toronto Subway.

[4] The Chicago Transit Authority's experimental cars have attained speeds of 72 miles per hour.

Vehicle Life. Here again, because lightweight equipment is relatively new, available data are insufficient to prove or disprove the
theory that heavyweight vehicles will last longer. One intuitively
associates durability with heaviness, but in this case it could be
unjustified. It would seem that many transit vehicles last longer
than is desirable anyway, when social acceptability, aesthetics,
and technological improvements are considered.

Methods of Reducing Weight. Reductions in car body weight can
result from substituting aluminum or stainless steel for the denser
carbon steel ordinarily used in car construction, or from the use
of sandwich-type construction in which inner and outer walls of
light alloy are held together by hard foam materials. Designs in
the drawing board stage also take advantage of lightweight structural techniques developed in the aircraft industry. In general,
these weight reductions can be achieved only at the expense of
structural strength (particularly buffing strength) or an increase
in the total price of the car. Of the two, the former provides the
stronger argument for the use of heavy vehicles.

Significant weight reductions are possible in trucks and motors,
however, which will not affect the ability of the car to resist buckling forces. Tests are currently being run on experimental cars
using trucks which are on the average 9 to 11,000 pounds lighter
than conventional trucks. Even for the heavier vehicles, this represents a weight reduction of more than 20 per cent (excluding any
reductions made in the car body) and a corresponding reduction in
the annual electric power costs. These weight reductions can be
attributed largely to the transition from the use of outboard bearings (which protrude over the outboard sides of the wheels) to inboard bearings (which are mounted between the wheels).

4.3 Performance Characteristics

The acceleration, deceleration, and maximum speed capabilities
of rail transit vehicles constitute performance characteristics of
particular interest to us here. These characteristics should and
do vary from one operating property to another. The maximum
speed appropriate for the vehicles on one property may be overly
adequate for those on the next, while the requirements for acceleration ability may at the same time be quite similar. One would
not expect average speeds to be the same for two lines, one of
which spaced stations a quarter of a mile apart, the other one
mile apart. It is essential to realize, then, that there is no uni-
versal set of performance characteristics which will provide the
most economical, efficient, and attractive service for any and
every line. A maximum speed capability in excess of that which
can be attained between the majority of stations is basically inefficient, regardless of how attractive it may sound. The required
performance characteristics for efficient operation of a rail transit

vehicle can thus be determined only after both the location
of the route and the nature of the intended service have been established.

The determination of desirable performance characteristics
is a two-stage process. The first stage involves the selection of
rates of acceleration, deceleration and maximum speed. For two
reasons the major criterion here is maximization of average
speed. First, maximizing average speed is desirable from the
standpoint of the passenger, for if the public is to be completely
satisfied with the service, the performance of the vehicle should
at least equal or better that of the automobile with respect to average speed. Second, increasing the average speed decreases
the number of vehicles required to service a line of given length,
thereby economizing both on capital outlay, and the wages paid to
operating crews.

The average speed attained depends on acceleration, deceleration, maximum speed, and station separation, and can be computed by a straightforward application of the basic laws of motion.
Figure 4.2 illustrates this in graphical form.

As pointed out earlier, the maximum speed should not be greater than that which can be attained between the bulk of the stations.
This would imply that the most efficient operation is obtained when
stations are evenly spaced. Since station separations are generally not equal, but tend to increase as one moves farther from the
central city, the use of skip-stop operation in areas where stations
are closely spaced may result in a more even distribution of station stops.

Maximum acceleration and deceleration rates are generally limited by one of three considerations: the physical limit of the fric-
tional force which can be developed between wheel and track, passenger comfort, or, in the case of acceleration, power costs. Under normal operation conditions, acceleration and deceleration
rates are most often limited by passenger comfort considerations.
Tests have shown that a combination of both acceleration and the
rate of change of acceleration determines passenger comfort.[5]
The comfort limit for acceleration rate is generally accepted as
from 3 to 4 mph per second, 3 mph per second being in common
use today. The limit for rate of change of acceleration is taken to
be 7 feet per second[3]. These limits correspond roughly to those
attained by the well-known (PCC) streetcar. The same limits are
used for both acceleration and deceleration (although it is recog-
nized that deceleration to a stopped position is not identical with
the reverse situation), generally with provision for an emergency
deceleration ability of 4 mph per second.

---

[5] C. F. Hirshfeld, Disturbing Effects of Horizontal Acceleration,
Electric Railway Presidents' Conference Committee, Bulletin 3,
New York, 1932.

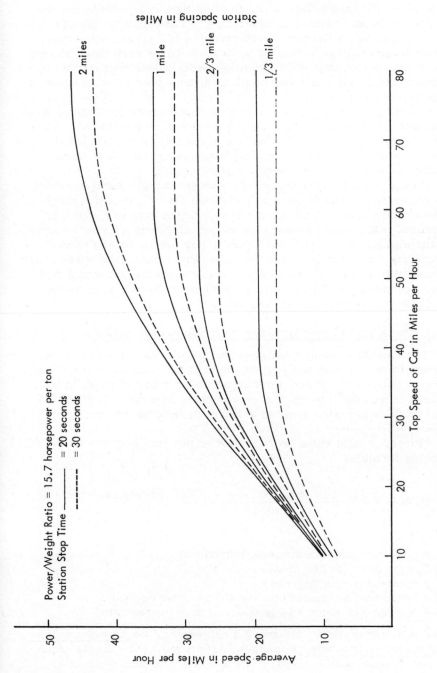

Figure 4.2. Relationship between top speed, station spacing, and average speed.

The second stage in determining performance characteristics involves selecting power/weight ratios that will provide the desired speed and rates of acceleration. The following factors are relevant to this selection: maximum speed, acceleration rate, distribution voltage at the train, train running resistance at various speeds, track profile and alignment, wheel diameter and moment of inertia, number of motors, and over-all efficiency of the motors and gears.

Given this information, the required power/weight ratio can be computed for various points along the route under study.[6]   Where very high power/weight ratios are needed at only a few points, economics may dictate accepting lower performance at those points in favor of lower over-all power costs.

Figure 4.3 indicates the effect of power/weight ratio in vehicle performance. The sloping line through the origin of the graph shows the effect of limiting the acceleration rate to 3 mph per second. One should note that even vehicles with a power/weight ratio as high as the 15.7 horsepower per ton shown (B) cannot maintain maximum acceleration throughout the entire speed range. This vehicle could accelerate at an average rate of about 3 mph per second up to 30 mph, but it could average only 1.3 mph per second in accelerating up to 60 mph.

4.4 The Effect of Performance on Equipment Requirements

The amount of equipment required to service a given line depends in the first instance upon the peak demand for transportation. This peak demand determines the number of cars, in trains, which must pass a point in a given period of time. (Notice that the number of trains passing per unit of time is the inverse of

---

[6] Power/weight ratio (in horsepower per ton) is given by the following formula:

$$P/W = \frac{2.67 \times 10^{-3} \ (r - 20G - g - 100a)}{1000e} \quad \text{horsepower per ton}$$

where

  r = train resistance (in pounds per ton).
  G = gradient (in per cent).
  g = curvature (in degrees).
  a = desired acceleration rate (in mph per second).
  e = over-all motor and gear efficiency (in per cent).

See William W. Hay, "Railroad Engineering," in American Civil Engineering Practice, Robert W. Abbett (ed.) (New York: John Wiley & Sons, 1956), p. 84. The effect of moment of inertia, number, and voltage of motors on "e" is discussed in more detail on pp. 82-85.

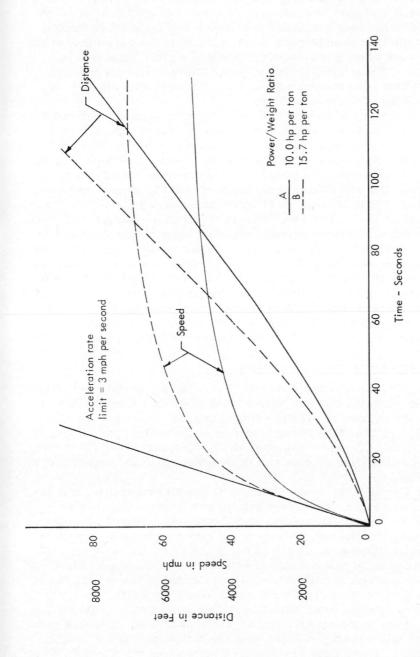

Figure 4.3. Equipment performance curves.
Source: Chicago Transit Authority.

headway. Thus, depending upon the number of cars in each train, the number of cars passing may be subject to the limitations on minimum headway discussed in Chapter 5.) As average running speed (including turnaround time) increases, the possibility of the same cars passing the same point within a given time also increases. Thus, vehicle performance characteristics, through their effect upon running speed, can affect the total number of cars required to service a line.

For purposes of illustration let us assume peak demand requires that trains pass on a two-minute headway over a period of one hour; that is, it requires that 30 trains pass over the line during one hour. The maximum number of different trains thus required is 30. If the first train because of high average speed can make a complete trip and return to the starting point in time to make the 30th run, however, only 29 different trains are required; if it returns to make the 29th run, only 28 trains are required; and so on.

The effect of higher average speed on equipment requirements is thus subject to qualifications. In order to take advantage of an increase in average speed, total round-trip time must be such as to allow a second pass during the peak hour. In general, higher average speeds are attained on the longer lines, and one train may not get a second pass at the rush-hour crowds. On short routes, where stations are generally more frequent, the average speed often cannot be varied sufficiently to alter equipment requirements.

4.5 Car Capacity and Dimensions

The capacity of a rapid transit line is the simple product of the number of trains that can pass a given point in a given period of time, the number of cars per train, and the capacity of each individual car. The next chapter will discuss the first two factors in some detail. In this section we shall be concerned with the third, that is, with those elements of design that affect the capacity of an individual car.

Car Length. On most existing rail transit properties, car dimensions (length, width, and height) are fixed by the clearance limits for existing structures and alignments. Where new lines are being constructed, moreover, it may be advisable to adhere to the car dimensions required for other lines, so as to maintain flexibility in the interchange of equipment. Even where this is not the case, length in particular may be limited to that which can be handled by existing repair and maintenance facilities.

Where existing conditions do not dictate maximum car length, an analysis of the positive and negative advantages of longer car lengths is necessary to determine the optimum. As car length increases, fewer cars are required for a given train length. This tends to lower the initial cost of a given amount of capacity since fewer trucks, motors, and controls are required. Where   crew

size is dependent on the number of cars, fewer guards are required. In addition, coupling costs decrease, because there are
fewer units to be coupled. The advantages of longer length are
thus positive with respect to both initial and operating costs.

The negative advantages of longer length relate to weight and
alignment considerations. Returning to the analogy of the car
structure as a simply supported beam, one sees that the bending
moment increases as the second power of the length. Greater
strength is thus required with increasing length, and this increases car weight per foot of length. As car length increases,
shearing stresses also increase, so that it is necessary to provide additional material at the critical points above doorways.
This results in a higher car and greater vertical clearance requirements which may be very costly in subway construction.

If one considers only the first cost of the cars themselves, the
cost per unit capacity appears to decrease with increasing car
lengths up to approximately 85 feet.[7] This may be reduced somewhat by the effect of vertical clearance considerations on construction cost, since increasing car length involves larger curve radii
(if speed is not to be reduced) and thus higher construction and
right-of-way costs.

Car Width. The same remarks concerning existing clearances
apply here as well. Past experience indicates that two-abreast
seating using 38-inch seats provides adequate comfort. For newer
equipment using this arrangement car widths of about 10 feet
are common. Again, existing clearance limitations can rule out
such widths. In one case where existing clearances at platform
level were too confining, however, cars were built with sloping
sides so as to provide more width at seat level where it was most
essential.

Seat and Door Arrangement. The number of seats that should
be provided in a car of given dimensions depends on whether one
is maximizing capacity or comfort. The usage to which floor
space is put in one locale may be totally unacceptable in another.
It is admittedly difficult to approach this question analytically,
but its importance cannot be overestimated. Utilization of floor
space so as to maximize the number of seats may result in intol-
erable overcrowding of standees. On the other hand, if standing
capacity is maximized at the expense of seating, many of the passengers for whom this capacity has been provided may not use the
facility because they cannot get a seat.

In Table 4.1 data for several transit properties show the relationship between car capacity and passenger comfort (per cent

---

[7] This figure does not take into account the operating and maintenance savings mentioned above. In the case of operating economies, most properties already operate on a basis where crew
size is independent of train length.

Table 4.1. Sample Car-Capacity Data

Car	Maximum Load			80% of Maximum Load		
	Percentage Seated	Passengers per Square Foot	Passengers per Foot	Percentage Seated	Passengers per Square Foot	Passengers per Foot
Cleveland	36	0.34	3.1	45	0.27	2.5
Chicago	38	0.35	2.7	47	0.28	2.2
Toronto	28	0.42	3.8	35	0.33	3.1
Philadelphia*	29	0.43	3.4	38	0.34	2.8
New York (IRT)	22	0.50	3.9	27	0.40	3.1
(BMT)	16	0.56	5.0	21	0.46	4.0

*Market-Frankford Line

seated) in a very general way. These data are also plotted in Figure 4.4 and are shown for both maximum loading conditions and 80 per cent of this maximum level. The 80 per cent figure is considered most desirable from the point of view of passenger crowding. The relevant measure of capacity in this respect is passengers per square foot of car floor area, referred to elsewhere as the "passenger loading coefficient." (The unit of measure, passengers per lineal foot of car length, is relevant to the discussion of track capacity in Chapter 5.) The variation shown for these measures of passenger loading is largely a function of the seating arrangements used. High loadings, and thus a low proportion of seated passengers, are generally made possible by longitudinal seating arrangements (as in the New York cars). Lower loadings result from the use of transverse seating (Chicago or Cleveland cars), while intermediate values can be obtained by the use of both transverse and longitudinal seating (Toronto cars). With regard to the figures shown in Table 4.1, it should be noted that a passenger-loading coefficient of 0.15 passenger per square foot is approximately that required to give everyone a seat.

In addition to these considerations of passenger comfort and car capacity, the effect of seating arrangement on loading and unloading time (and thus on line capacity) is also important. Here again, it is necessary to substitute judgment for a lack of analytical data. In general, the following rules apply in determining seating and door arrangements:

1. Doors and seats should be arranged so as to minimize the distance between each seat and the nearest door. This may be accomplished by arranging seats so as to face the nearest exit. In the case of cars having only two doors to a side, they should be placed at the quarter points of the car.
2. Passenger exits should be accomplished with a minimum of disturbance to other passengers. For this reason, two-abreast seating is considered desirable for cars having transverse seating. In this situation the outside passenger pivots

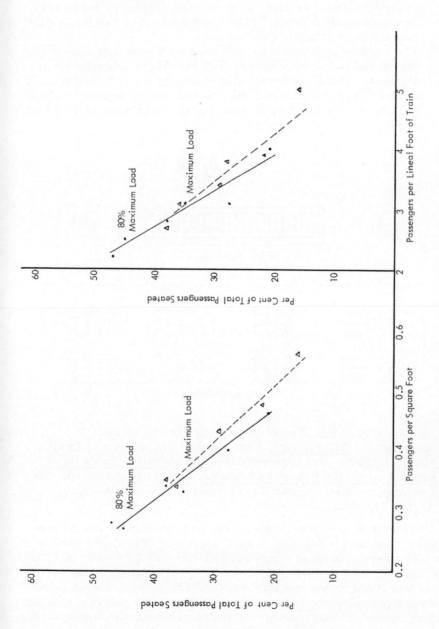

Figure 4.4. Maximum car capacity versus percentage seated.

in his seat to allow the inside passenger to pass by, whereas in three-abreast seating, it is usually necessary for at least one passenger to stand. (The arrangement of car (a) in Figure 4.5 is an exception to this case.)

3. The number of doors to be provided on a side depends on car length and on the average level of passenger interchange at stations. For a low level of interchange (as in Cleveland), a door ratio of 0.15 foot per foot of car seems adequate, while for high levels (such as in New York) a minimum of 0.25 foot per foot of car is necessary.

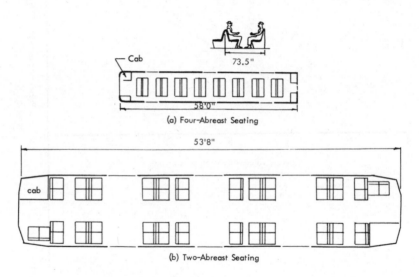

Figure 4.5. Proposed seating arrangements.
Sources: (a) Railway Age, October 3, 1960, p. 16; (b) Daniel, Mann, Johnson, and Mendenhall, A Comparative Analysis of Rapid Transit Equipment and Routes, Report prepared for the Los Angeles Metropolitan Transit Authority, Los Angeles, August 26, 1960.

The doors in use today are generally of the double-sliding type. Inward glide doors (similar to PCC streetcar doors) are used to a limited extent. Opening times range from 1 to 2 seconds and closing times from 2 to 3 seconds for each type. Many sliding door types are fitted with sensitized edges which cause the door to reopen if any resistance is encountered. From the safety standpoint this is desirable, but from the operational standpoint it becomes an easy matter for passengers to delay a train by deliberately pressing on the sensitized edge of the door. In this respect, folding doors tend to have a more positive closing action, although it is doubtful that they could be used for very heavy loading conditions. The provision of end doors is desirable in the event emergency exit is necessary. They may also be desirable to allow normal passenger movement between car units in order to achieve a more uniform distribution of passenger load between cars.

The Problem of Capacity and Comfort. The preceding sections have approached the questions of car performance and car capacity from two different standpoints: that of making the most efficient use of equipment and facilities, and that of maximizing the level of passenger comfort. With respect to car performance these two viewpoints are compatible; maximum average speed is desirable in each case. In the case of car capacity, however, they are opposed; maximizing the number of passengers per car tends to minimize comfort. The final design decisions which are made must reflect a compromise between quality of service on one hand and economical operation on the other. These decisions may have as important an effect on the success of a transit line as those which determine the actual location of the route.

Essentially, this is a problem of supply and demand, where a feedback exists through which demand is affected by supply. In urban areas where a substantial segment of the population has little choice but to use the transit system, this feedback effect of passenger comfort will be less pronounced than in areas where alternative forms of transportation are more readily available.

4.6 Heating, Ventilation, and Air Conditioning

The heating, ventilating, and air conditioning of transit cars affect both operating costs and passenger comfort. Air conditioning of rail transit equipment has become a particularly important consideration in the design of new vehicles.

Heating and Ventilation. Heating is generally provided by thermostatically or manually controlled electric heaters. Heaters should be used sparingly during the peak hour, so as to keep peak power demand to a minimum.[8] For this reason, newly proposed systems may include some means of central control to ensure that heaters are turned off when the system-wide power demand for traction is at its maximum. (One method which has been considered is the use of "ship-to-shore" type communications through which the motor man receives instructions regarding the use of heaters.) Fortunately, the need for heating is least during the peak hours, so limiting the use of heaters at these hours has a less serious effect on passenger comfort.

---

[8] Keep in mind that transit system power costs are usually determined by the peak demand for power as well as the total power used.

The conventional method of ventilation in rail transit vehicles involves fans and duct systems housed in a double-roof structure. Power costs for driving the fans are not significant relative to power costs for heating and air conditioning.

Air Conditioning. Thus far, there has been no widespread use of air conditioning in operating transit cars. High cost has been the most important factor working against its introduction. Estimates of initial costs of equipment range up to $20,000 per car, with annual operating and maintenance costs of approximately $1,000. The problem of power cost is serious, too. The demand on an air conditioning system is greatest during the rush hour when the peak load is already being drawn on the power system. The result is to raise the cost of all power delivered to the transit operation. In addition, power consumption of the air conditioning system is in itself significant, being on the order of 20 kilowatts per car, or 5 to 10 per cent of total power requirements.

It is doubtful in any case that air conditioning can function well in rapid transit operations. Experience in New York (where passenger loadings are admittedly extreme) indicates that the high cost is not justified by any substantial increase in passenger comfort.[9] On properties where the doors are opened and closed less frequently, this might not be the case. An argument might also be advanced for equipping only a portion of the vehicle fleet with air conditioning. These cars could be used during the off-peak hours when the air-conditioning equipment would function more efficiently, and at a time when the attraction of more patronage is of prime importance.

4.7 Rubber-Wheeled Vehicles

The discussion thus far has been restricted to conventional steel-wheeled vehicles traveling on steel tracks. There is much current interest, however, in the rubber-tired transit vehicles operating in the Paris Métro. The use of similar vehicles has even been proposed for a Los Angeles rapid transit system. In Chapter 2 there were some remarks concerning the track structure necessary to accommodate these vehicles. The following section discusses the vehicles themselves and how their capabilities differ from those of conventional rail transit vehicles.

Basic Differences. The only essential difference between steel-wheeled and rubber-wheeled transit vehicles is in their trucks. The basic function of the truck on a steel-wheeled vehicle is merely to transmit load to the track structure. The track structure itself provides guidance for both normal running and changes in

---

[9] Mr. R. G. Welch of the New York City Transit Authority indicated that air conditioning composed of 6 two-ton machines per car failed to do an adequate job under New York conditions. Letter to R. M. Soberman dated July 5, 1961.

direction (switching). For rubber-wheeled vehicles the truck
must also provide a guidance capability, the nature of the wheel
being such that it cannot be guided by the track on which it is
running. In actual practice, moreover, the rubber-wheeled
truck provides one guidance mechanism for normal running and
another for switching. The former makes use of horizontal rubber guide wheels which bear against a raised section of the required special track structure. This raised section also incorporates a positive derailment stop. Switching is accomplished by
the use of conventional steel-flanged wheels. During normal running the steel wheels make no contact; during switching operations
they carry the entire weight of the vehicle while the rubber wheels
hang free. Figure 4.6 illustrates a truck designed to operate in
this way.

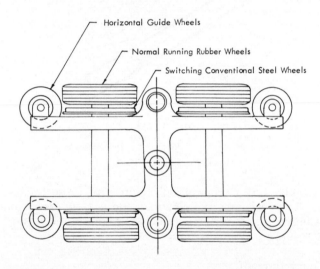

Figure 4.6. Proposed rubber-wheeled truck.
Source: Daniel, Mann, Johnson, and Mendenhall, A Comparative Analysis of Rapid Transit Equipment and Routes.

Noise Level. The exterior noise levels produced by rubber-
tired vehicles have already been discussed. At the present stage
of development, however, very little can be said about interior
noise levels. In Figure 4.7, an estimated range of noise levels
has been plotted for purposes of comparison with measurements
taken in PCC streetcars and large piston-engine airliners. These
sound levels have been plotted for the range of frequencies used in
normal speech, as it has been suggested that interference with
conversation provides a good measure of the acceptability of an

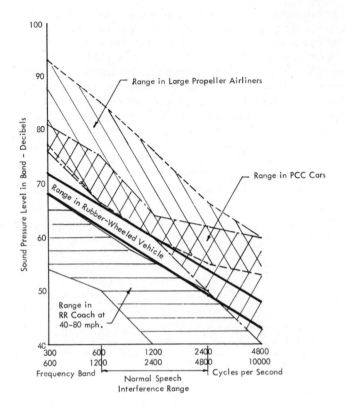

Figure 4.7. Comparison of interior noise levels.
Source: Bolt Beranek and Newman Inc., Considerations of
Noise Control for the Proposed Los Angeles Mass Rapid
Transit System, Los Angeles, 1960.

acoustic environment.[10]

Comfort. It seems reasonable to expect some increase in
riding comfort through the use of rubber-tired vehicles. How significant this increase will be is difficult to estimate since there
are examples of well-maintained steel-wheeled systems in which
riding comfort is in no sense objectionable. In the case of rubber-
wheeled vehicles, lateral bounce due to the horizontal tires may
easily prove objectionable. Both noise level and riding comfort
are factors, moreover, that will be difficult to evaluate in any
economic analysis comparing steel-wheeled and rubber-tired vehicles.

[10] Bolt Beranek and Newman Inc., Considerations of Noise
Control for the Proposed Los Angeles Mass Rapid Transit System,
Report No. 712, Los Angeles, 1960, p. 24.

Performance. In addition to the advantages already mentioned, rubber-tired vehicles are often said to have better acceleration ability and grade ability. These characteristics are attributed to the much higher friction coefficients that can be developed between rubber and concrete as compared to those developed between steel and steel. The ranges for these values is from only 0.12 to 0.35 for steel wheels on steel rail, but from 0.30 to 0.90 for rubber wheels on concrete.[11] The apparent advantages this offers requires more careful examination. Some of the more important considerations in this regard are listed now:

1. Since rolling resistances for pneumatic tires are considerably higher than for steel wheels, the power/weight ratio necessary for a given level of performance is greater for rubber-wheeled than for steel-wheeled vehicles. Weight remaining the same, therefore, the rubber-tired vehicle will have higher power costs.

2. The use of rubber-tired vehicles will undoubtedly reduce the vibratory stresses transmitted to the car structure and truck. This may result in a considerable saving in car weight for a Métro car equal in size to a conventional car. Since these vibratory stresses are of a secondary nature, however, it seems doubtful that the weight reduction will be sufficient to compensate entirely for the higher power/weight ratio.

3. Acceleration is generally limited by passenger comfort considerations and this limit can be attained by conventional steel-wheeled vehicles. In addition the power costs associated with using the higher acceleration ability of the Métro car may be prohibitive when the size of the necessary traction motors is considered.

4. The greater ability of the Métro car to handle grades can conceivably be a factor under two conditions: where the route is located in hilly terrain, and in transition zones between underground and at-level or elevated operation. In the first case the use of steeper grades may save route length, while in the second case savings in construction and right-of-way costs may be realized. In general, however, grades are rarely so steep that steel wheels will slip.

5. Figures are not currently available to compare the maintenance costs for rubber- and steel-wheeled vehicles. It seems reasonable, however, to expect lower maintenance costs for the Métro cars because of reduced vibration. On the other hand the cost of wheel wear and replacement should be higher

---

[11] Daniel, Mann, Johnson, and Mendenhall, A Comparative Analysis of Rapid Transit System Equipment and Routes, Report prepared for the Los Angeles Metropolitan Transit Authority, Los Angeles, August 1960, p. 32.

than for conventional wheels.[12]   Since the load-carrying capacity of rubber wheels is less than steel wheels, a larger number of rubber wheels may also be required.

The foregoing considerations will carry different weights depending upon the nature and location of the proposed route and upon relative maintenance and power costs. In summary, noise level and ability to accelerate on grades are factors which might favor the use of Métro type cars; low power costs, lower maintenance costs, and simpler track structure are factors which tend to favor conventional steel-wheeled vehicles. Where obtaining public acceptance of a rail transit proposal is important, the novelty of a rubber-tired rapid transit vehicle might also be a significant consideration. In areas where conventional rail transit already exists, or where a proposed route can make use of abandoned railroad lines, flexibility considerations will probably dictate the use of conventional steel-wheeled vehicles.

4.8 Automation

The automatic control of rail transit vehicles is currently being considered for both existing and proposed rail transit facilities. Chapter 2 discussed the signal system component of a completely automated rail transit system. This section discusses automation of the vehicle itself.

Completely automatic operation is unquestionably feasible from the technological standpoint. At least two test installations of automatic train control are now in operation: one involving a two-terminal shuttle service in New York City, the other involving a trial section of elevated line in London. Other test installations will have gone in as this book is being written.

The economic feasibility of automation is not yet so apparent. On the one hand, the ultimate costs of automation have not been accurately determined. Not only is there a wide range of technically feasible automation techniques, but also none of the requisite equipment has yet been produced in quantity. On the other hand, the benefits of automatic control have not been clearly identified either. The general assumption has been that automation will be accompanied by decreased labor costs, economies in electric power consumption, and greater safety at closer headways. The extent to which such benefits might actually materialize depends very much upon the circumstances.

Labor Cost Savings. A first step in estimating the possible

[12] The Los Angeles study estimates wheel costs of 0.14 cent per wheel-mile for rubber wheels, and 0.21 cent per wheel-mile for rubber sandwich steel wheels used on PCC cars. (The latter, however, are not used on any rail transit property.) A comparable figure for steel wheels is 0.025 cent per wheel-mile.

effect of automation on labor costs is to determine the scale of the
costs with which we are dealing. As an example, consider an
eight-car train operating with a two-man crew at an average speed
of 20 miles per hour. Suppose also that the men are paid $2.70
per hour and that because of scheduling and union work rules each
man actually works only 4 hours of an 8-hour work day. (Reasons
for this are discussed in Chapter 6.) Train labor costs are then
6.8 cents per car-mile during the peak hour. If we assume the
train would be reduced to four cars during off-peak hours, the labor costs would then increase to 13.5 cents per car-mile. Presumably, these are the costs that can be saved by automation.

The picture is actually less simple. Removal of a two-man
crew could not be credited entirely to automation. In the first
place, all proposals for automation thus far considered have rec-
ommended the use of an attendant, for reasons which have been
stated as follows:

> It seems imprudent to leave without human presence, a high-
> speed train containing several hundred passengers, were it
> only to cope with mechanical incidents and with obstructions of
> the running track. [13]

If this is the case, automation could at best be credited with reducing labor costs by only 3.4 cents per car-mile during peak
hours and 6.8 cents per car-mile during off-peak hours, given the
previous cost assumptions.

Even in the case where a train operates unattended, it is incor-
rect to credit automation with saving all of the present labor costs.
Though not usual practice, one-man manual operation is readily
possible today. Such difficulties as it may pose can be overcome
by the use of full-width motormen's cabs, mirrors, or even
closed-circuit television—all of which are relatively minor innovations when compared to automatic control. Under the best conditions in each case, therefore, manual operation requires only one
man per train while automatic operation requires none, a net saving of but one man per train.

Other considerations relative to labor costs are more favorable
to automation. For instance, it is reasonable to assume that as
automatic control systems are perfected, their unit costs will go
down. On the other hand, unit labor costs should continue to increase. Over the life of a facility, automation may thus result in
lower annual costs of train operation despite its less favorable
position now. The nontechnological obstacles to reducing the size
of crews on manually controlled trains is another consideration,
too. As discussed in Chapter 6, these obstacles take the form of

---

[13] Société Autonyme Française d'Etudes de Gestion et d'Entre-
prises (SAFEGE), Overhead Suspended Rapid Transit, Paris, 1959,
p. 91.

long-established work practices which by their nature prevent the efficient operation of a labor-intensive transit system. These practices cannot be changed, if at all, without excessive bad publicity, arbitration, and cost. Fewer restraining precedents would be established on a completely automated system, and this could weigh heavily in favor of automation for any new lines.

Power Economies. It has already been pointed out that electric power costs depend upon the peak demand for power as well as the total quantity used. It has been suggested that with automatic control the operation of all vehicles in a system could be controlled according to an optimized program, so that peak power demand would be minimized. As an example, it might be possible to program a master schedule so that all trains in the system would not be accelerating at the same time. Similarly, it might be possible to make better use of regenerative braking (in which the braking energy of the car is put back into the power supply system) by balancing the total number of trains accelerating with those decelerating at any one time. All things considered, however, power economies obtained in this manner would probably not be substantial. In particular, the most desirable operating schedule for power economy will probably not be the most desirable for meeting traffic demands.

Safety at Closer Headways.[14] It has already been suggested in Chapter 2 that automatic control would permit closer headways, because it would eliminate the reaction time necessary when human operators respond to various conditions. Where desired headways are less than those which can be accommodated by manual control systems, therefore, automation may be a means of increasing the capacity of a route.

Even at existing headways the use of automatic control may significantly increase the safety of operation. Accidents involving rear-end collisions, for instance, have generally resulted from the failure of the motormen to observe a signal. Many derailments have resulted from excessive speeds on curves. The use of automatic control can eliminate both of these errors. In the first case, when some malfunction of the control system causes a signal to be disobeyed, a second signal to stop the train can be relayed to the train in less time than a motorman could react after having realized such an error. Protection from derailment can also be greatly improved by the provision of positive speed control equipment on curves. Accident savings of this sort should be taken into account when considering the cost of automation.

4.9 Vehicle Costs

One of the problems encountered in comparing transit vehicles

---

[14] Headway is defined as the time-spacing between successive trains.

and their costs is lack of standardization. The standards often
used in comparing initial costs—such as costs per passenger, per
seat, per pound, or per foot of length—are generally inadequate.
Costs per passenger may vary significantly from one property to
another, for example, even though equipment is identical for each,
because of a difference in the level of comfort (in this case, density of loading) acceptable in each city. One must be careful,
therefore, to adopt units of comparison which have some general
significance.

Capacity and performance are the two characteristics of rail
transit vehicles which are most important to the planner and transportation engineer. The most general measure of capacity is car
floor area. In comparing costs, then, the price per unit area can
best be used. This can in turn be translated into specific capacity,
depending on the level of comfort acceptable to the public in the
particular area for which the service is designed. A general measure of performance is power/weight ratio. As discussed in Section 4.3 of this chapter, this ratio determines the combinations of
acceleration ability and maximum speed which are possible. These
measures of capacity and performance characteristics can in turn
be related by means of the weight per unit floor area.

Initial Costs. Rail transit vehicles purchased within the last
five or six years range in cost from $67,000 to $121,000 per unit.[15]
This variation is due to differences in weight, power, capacity,
and to the use in some cars of stainless steel and other materials
not requiring painted surfaces. Table 4.2 is a tabulation of these
various characteristics for representative rail transit equipment
currently in operation on this continent. Table 4.3 shows ranges
of capacity and performance costs for both lightweight and heavyweight equipment.

Operating Costs. Operating and maintenance costs for rail
transit equipment are discussed in Chapter 6. It is interesting to
note here, however, that additional capital expense may reduce
later maintenance and operating costs. The new transit vehicles
presently being purchased in Philadelphia are an example of this.
An additional initial expenditure of $7,000 for each of these cars
has been justified on the basis of average annual savings of $428
(discounted at 5 per cent for 35 years). For these stainless steel
cars, the savings result from the elimination of painting and cor-
rosion repair. In addition, an initial cost differential is also justified by lighter weights.

---

[15] For purposes of comparison, the cost of a new 50-passenger
diesel bus is $25,000 to $40,000. The economic life of a bus is
perhaps half that of a rail car.

Table 4.2. Summary of Transit Vehicle Data

| | New York | | Toronto | Cleveland | Chicago | Philadelphia |
	IND	IRT				
Length	60'-2"	51'-1"	57'-2"	48'-6"	48'-0"	55'-4"
Width	10'-0"	8'-10"	10'-4"	10'-4"	9'-4"	9'-0"
Height	12'-2"	11'-11"	11'-11"	11'-9"	11' 10"	12'-9"
Body Weight (In 1000 pounds)	45.7	35.9	42.0	32.6	25.4	25.9
Truck Weight (In 1000 pounds)	38.4	38.4	42.3	22.0	16.8	22.6
Total Empty Car Weight (In 1000 pounds)	84.1	74.3	84.3	54.6	42.2	48.5
Horsepower	400	400	260	220	220	400
Horsepower per Ton of Empty Weight	9.5	10.7	6.2	8.1	10.2	16.5
Seats	50	44	62	54	51	56
Square Feet of Floor Area (*Indicates approximate value)	535*	400*	525*	445	368	445*
Maximum Passengers	250	200	220	196	181	190
Pounds per Foot	1395	1520	1475	1120	902	930
Pounds per Square Foot	157	186	160	121	115	109
Maximum Speed (In miles per hour)	45	45	47	55	50	55
Initial Acceleration (In mph per second)	2.5	2.5	2.3	2.3	3.0	3.0
Year Purchased	1960	1960	1952	1958	1957	1960
Cost (In $1000)	119.3	106.6	90.0	77.5	67.0	92.5
Dollars per Square Foot	223	267	171	174	182	208
Dollars per Seat	2390	2420	1450	1440	1310	1650

Table 4.3. Ranges of Rail Transit Vehicle Capacity and Performance Costs

	Lightweight	Heavyweight
Pounds per Square Foot of Floor Space	110-130	160-190
Cost in Dollars per Square Foot	180-210[*]	170[†]-265
Power/Weight Ratio in Horsepower per Ton	7.9/16.0	6.6/10.6

[*] This high figure is for stainless steel construction.
[†] This figure is for equipment not built in the United States.

Chapter 5

CAPACITY

The passenger-carrying capacity of a transportation system can have an important effect upon its costs. This is particularly true of modes of transportation with relatively high fixed costs, a condition which Chapter 6 shows is typical of most rail transit systems. These costs are, of course, important determinants of the ability of a system to compete in the transportation market. Chapter 7 discusses this.

The question of passenger-carrying capacity also becomes important in urban transportation because of its effect upon land use, that is, right-of-way requirements. The removal of large amounts of developable land from urban tax rolls to build modern highway facilities has recently aroused particular concern over this aspect of the capacity question.

Passenger-carrying capacity is thus a primary consideration in assessing the capabilities of rail transit relative to other modes of urban transportation.

5.1 Determinants of Capacity

The hourly capacity of a single transit track is determined by the number of trains which can pass a given point during one hour and the number of passengers carried in each train. This relationship can be expressed by the equation

$$Q = \frac{60k'L}{H} = \frac{60k'nl}{H} \tag{5.1}$$

where

Q = capacity (in passengers per hour passing any given point on a single track)

H = headway (in minutes[1])

k' = loading coefficient (in passengers per foot of train length[2])

[1] A headway of 2 minutes corresponds to a volume of 30 trains per hour.

[2] Note the difference between k' and k, the loading coefficient in passengers per square foot of car floor area discussed in Chapters 4 and 6. As defined here, k' is approximately equal to k multiplied by the interior width of the cars.

61

1 = length of each car (in feet)
n = number of cars per train
L = total train length = nl

Equation 5.1 shows that running trains of the longest possible
length at minimum headways would theoretically maximize capacity. In the limiting case one would obtain maximum capacity with
a continuous, conveyor-type system in which headways were effectively zero, and train lengths were equal to the total length of
route. As a practical matter, limitations on the available supply
of equipment and on minimum standards in the quality of service
provided render this solution unacceptable. These factors thus
have an important bearing upon the capacity question.

The following equation indicates the general relationship between
headway, equipment requirements, and average speed. For a headway of H and an average speed of $\overline{V}'$, the distance spacing between
trains is given by $H\overline{V}'$. The total number of trains required per
mile of route, neglecting turnaround time, equals the reciprocal of
this value. Expressed in equation form:

$$N = \frac{60n}{H\overline{V}'} \qquad\qquad (5.2)$$

where

N = approximate number of cars required per mile of single
track (where n = number of cars per train)
$\overline{V}'$ = average train speed in feet per second

Equation 5.2 shows that reducing headways to increase capacity
can usually be accomplished only at the expense of an increase in
equipment requirements. The alternative would be to increase average train speed; but (as will be explained below) a reduction in
headway usually requires a decrease in speed. The problem of capacity, then, is not merely one of determining the maximum number of passengers which can be carried past a point in a given
amount of time. Rather, it is one of determining this number for a
given quantity of equipment and with an acceptable quality of service (average speed). Some of the more important factors to be
considered in analyzing this problem are discussed below.

Headway. The basic alternatives in selecting a desirable headway are to use short, slow trains at frequent intervals or longer,
faster trains at less frequent intervals. The optimum solution depends on many factors, of which station spacing is probably the
most significant. Greater station separations allow higher average speeds and fewer trains. In many cases, however, this adjustment of train speed, length, and headway so as to maximize
equipment utilization becomes a purely academic problem. Traffic demand may require use of the longest possible trains (usually

determined by station platform lengths), while performance capabilities of the train itself (acceleration, deceleration, and maximum speed) will dictate the average speeds which can be attained. In such cases, the reduction of headways between trains of given length and performance characteristics becomes the major problem.

The problem of reducing headways has always been of interest in the transit industry. It has provided much of the incentive for the development and subsequent improvement in transit signaling systems. Of course, modern block signaling is also designed to maintain a safe distance (that is, headway) between the successive trains in any section of line. This distance is some function of the maximum train speed which will be reached in that section. In sections containing no stations, for example, the equation relating minimum safe headway to train speed is given by

$$h = t + \frac{L}{V} + \frac{2.03V}{d} \qquad\qquad (5.3)$$

For sections with stations

$$h = T + \frac{L}{V} + \frac{V}{2a} + \frac{5.05V}{2d} \qquad\qquad (5.4)$$

where

h = headway in seconds
t = time required for motorman reaction and brake operation in seconds
L = total train length in feet
T = station stop time in seconds
V = maximum train speed in feet per second
a = rate of acceleration in feet per second^2
d = rate of deceleration in feet per second^2

These equations are developed fully in Appendix A (as Equations A.2b and A.4). They show that where block signal systems are in use, smaller headways will be obtained largely at the expense of average speed. With the more sophisticated block signal systems, particularly those using speed control wayside signals or cab signals, this reduction in average speed may not be too significant.

Train Length. The time required for the train to travel its own length, denoted by L/V, may be a significant factor in operating with short headways and slow-moving trains. Therefore, if train length is increased, a corresponding increase in train speed is usually necessary if capacity is not to be reduced.

Loading Coefficient. The effect of car dimensions and seating and door arrangements on the value of k' used in Equation 5.1 has already been discussed in Chapter 4. It was pointed out there that increases in the value of this loading coefficient are generally obtained at the expense of passenger comfort. Values of k' range from about 2.2 to 4.0 passengers per foot of car length, depending upon car width and the severity of loading conditions. It should also be noted that high loading coefficients will usually be accompanied by longer station stop times due to the slower rate of loading. This will in turn result in increased headways.

Average Speed. Equation 5.2 shows that average train speed affects equipment costs and is in addition an important measure of quality of service. The average speed that can actually be realized by a train depends upon its maximum speed, its rates of acceleration and deceleration, station stop time, the distance between stations, and the time required for turnaround.

Station Stop Time. Critical headway conditions occur in track sections containing stations because of the time between trains required for the station stop itself as well as for deceleration and acceleration. Station stop time also has a significant effect on the over-all average trip speeds that may be reached on a transit line. It has been correctly stated that

> The time required for the station stop is the most important of the various factors which influence [headway], and while the value of this factor is mainly dependent on the amount of traffic at the station considered, it is greatly influenced by the physical arrangement of the station, and also by the efficiency of the train and platform staff.[3]

Chapter 3 showed that the length of the station stop can be significantly influenced by the location and dimensions of platforms and passageways. In addition, the station stop time is itself dependent upon headway, since the number of passengers to be loaded per stop decreases with increasing train frequency.

Station stop time is thus an important factor. It influences both track capacity (through its effect on headway) and equipment costs (through its effect on average speed). It is a factor, moreover, that cannot be altered by improvements in the signal system.

5.2 Capacity Calculations

Equation 5.4 can be used to calculate the effect on capacity of variations in train length, maximum speed, station stop time, and rate of acceleration. It should be noted that this equation will tend to give conservative values for capacity, since in actual practice better headway-speed relationships can be obtained through the use of various speed control measures as explained in Appendix A.

Figure A.4 plots Equation 5.4 for various combinations of train

---

[3] H. G. Brown, "The Signalling of a Rapid Transit Railway," Journal of the Institution of Electrical Engineers, Vol. 52, No. 223, May 1, 1914, p. 550.

length, station stop time, and rate of acceleration.[4] The headway
determined from such a figure, together with an appropriate value
of k' can be substituted in Equation 5.1 to calculate capacity.[5]   Table 5.1 is a summary of such calculations for various train speeds
and lengths.   These use the data from Figure A.4 together with a

Table 5.1. Single-Track Passenger Capacity
(For T = 40 seconds, k' = 3.1 passengers per foot)

Running Speed (In miles per hour)	Average Acceler- ation (In mph per second)	Passengers per Hour		
		L = 400 feet	L = 500 feet	L = 600 feet
20	3.0	60,600	72,400	83,200
30	3.0	56,200	68,300	79,700
40	2.65	52,100	62,300	73,200
50	2.0	44,600	55,100	65,000

loading coefficient of 3.1 passengers per foot.   Average values of
acceleration (which generally decrease with increasing train speed)
are assumed to be those of Car B in Figure 4.3.
    The capacity figures in this table are higher than those reached
on operating transit lines.   One must distinguish, however, between
supply, as represented by capacity, and demand, as represented
by measured volumes.   These calculations are based on the use of
high-performance equipment (as represented by Figure 4.3), and
stations which are so designed as to result in uniform loading of
trains.   The calculations also assume that turnaround time is not
excessive or that adequate train storage facilities exist at the end
of the line.
    The foregoing is a general method of determining line capacity
for various combinations of train length, station stop times,   and
train performance.   In the usual case, however, such factors as
station separation and acceleration ability are fixed.[6]   Under these

---

[4] Figure A.4 assumes a constant deceleration of 3.0 mph per second, a rate which can be achieved by most new equipment without
significant increases in cost.

[5] For example, a train speed of 35 miles per hour, a train length
of 500 feet, and an average acceleration rate of 2.0 mph per second results in a headway of 88 seconds for a station stop time of
40 seconds.   This in turn produces a capacity of 20,500 k' passengers per hour.

[6] Note that while station spacing does not appear as a factor in
Figure 5.1 it is implicitly assumed in the selection of a maximum
train speed (for given acceleration and deceleration).

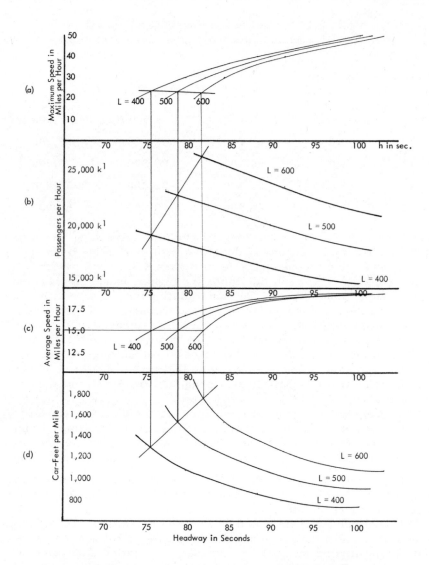

Figure 5.1. Optimum combinations of headway and train length.

circumstances the capacity problem reduces to one of determining that combination of train speed and length which will (1) maximize capacity with a given amount of equipment, or (2) provide a given capacity with a minimum amount of equipment.

Figure 5.1 illustrates one method of determining this optimum combination and helps also to explain the complex interrelationship between the various factors which are involved. Figure 5.1a plots minimum headway versus speed for trains of various length, assuming a station stop time of 40 seconds.[7] Figure 5.1b plots capacities corresponding to these curves. Figure 5.1c plots average speeds by combining the maximum speed for each train length and headway with station stop time, assuming a station separation of one-half mile. Figure 5.1d then shows the equipment required to meet these conditions.

In using such figures, one would first establish minimum acceptable average speeds or train frequency. For example, the condition that average speed must be no less than 15 miles per hour excludes from consideration all points in Figure 5.1 to the left of line x-x (as established in Figure 5.1c). Projecting from one figure to another, one can select that combination of train length and speed which meets this condition and still provides the highest capacity with the available equipment. Similar sets of figures can be drawn for different assumed station stop times (and for different station separations if this factor is variable) to determine the most probable range of values for train length and speed.

5.3 The Effect of Automation

With new developments in the field of automation it may ultimately be possible to achieve headways which are completely independent of train speed. In a completely automated system, for example, a train would be concerned not with the location of the preceding train but with the action being initiated by the preceding train. In this case, headways might approach the theoretical minimum derived in Appendix A, Equation A.1; namely

$$h = T + 2\sqrt{\frac{L}{a}} + R \qquad\qquad (5.5)$$

where R is a margin of safety added to account for the time lag in communications between successive trains. Thus capacity could be increased without a corresponding reduction in service quality (average speed).

---

[7] A station stop time of 40 seconds has been assumed so as to be conservative in estimating capacity. This is well over the normal stop time in off-peak hours or at low-volume stations. It may understate stop time for peak hours at downtown stations, however, and these are the conditions under which capacity becomes a problem.

Chapter 6

RAIL TRANSIT COSTS

6.1 Introduction

The costs discussed thus far—namely, those relating to the provision of the supporting way, stations and terminals, signaling,
and vehicles—are capital costs and thus essentially fixed. That is,
for a particular facility and a given amount of equipment these
costs are practically independent of the extent to which the facility
is used. In contrast, the costs of maintaining facilities and equipment and the costs of operation are essentially variable costs; that
is, they do depend upon the extent to which the facility is used.

In the costing of transportation services it is possible, of course,
to think of all costs as being variable in the "long run." The term
"long run," as used in this sense, implies that investment in fixed
plant can be adjusted in accordance with transportation output. With
rail transit facilities, however, this sort of adjustment is not entirely possible. The initial investment in supporting way and stations is based on the peak-hour demand the system is intended to
meet. Should this total peak-hour demand fail to materialize,
these fixed investments cannot be substantially reduced. Even with
some increase in peak-hour demand the variation in these costs
may be insignificant, since characteristically the fixed plant of a
transit system will have some excess capacity.[1]

Variable costs are contrasted to such fixed costs in that any increment in service, regardless of the level of demand at which
this increment occurs, will result in some change in costs.[2] The
variable costs of rail transit operation pose a special problem.
Their true incremental variation depends upon many different factors, but the available cost and operating data are insufficient to
determine all of the relevant relationships. Thus, we must work

---

[1] This stems simply from indivisibilities in the range of capacities one can provide. A pair of transit tracks has a potential capacity which is considerably above that which most systems are
actually called upon to handle.

[2] For a further discussion of this problem, see Section B.1 of
Appendix B. See also John Meyer, Merton Peck, John Stenason,
and Charles Zwick, The Economics of Competition in the Transportation Industries (Cambridge: Harvard University Press, 1959),
Chapter 2.

largely with average rather than true incremental costs. As explained in Section B.1 of Appendix B, this necessarily introduces
some error in whatever cost predictions we make. Our ability to
determine even these average costs, moreover, is limited by the
small number of existing transit operations from which to draw
our data. It is important that the discussion which follows be read
with these facts in mind.

This chapter will deal with both the fixed and variable components of transit costs. Data drawn from five transit properties
form the basis for estimates of operating and maintenance costs
as a function of system output. These costs combined with the
costs of investment in plant and equipment then yield over-all costs.
These are summarized at the conclusion of the chapter in the form
of unit costs per passenger-mile and related to alternative levels
of rush-hour transportation produced.[3] The last part of the chapter also briefly examines the effect of certain service quality factors upon costs.

6.2 Maintenance of Way and Structures

Those costs associated with the maintenance of all the fixed facilities of a system—tracks, tunnels, bridges, buildings, power
distribution systems, signal and communication systems, and so
forth—are generally classed under the heading of "maintenance of
way and structures." They comprise from 10 to 15 per cent or
more of total operating and maintenance costs. All of those way
and structures costs would generally be found in the following set
of accounts:

Way and Structures

1. Ballast
2. Ties
3. Rails
4. Rail Fastenings and Joints
5. Special Trackwork
6. Electric Track Switch (mechanical maintenance only)
7. Track and Roadway Labor and Miscellaneous Track Expenses
8. Track Grinding
9. Way, Shop Expense

---

[3] The cost per unit of transportation (i.e., the passenger-mile or
the trip) rather than the total cost of system operation is the critical factor in producing transportation under competitive conditions.
More particularly, it is the cost per unit of rush-hour transportation that is critical for urban rail transit systems. Because of
service quality disadvantages (as discussed further in Chapter 8),
they find their principal usefulness during only these 4 hours of
each working day.

10. Paving
11. Cleaning Track
12. Removal of Snow and Ice
13. Ventilating Equipment
14. Escalator Equipment
15. Water Removal (sumps)
16. Subway Bridges over Tracks
17. Signals and Interlockers, Electric Switches
18. Third Rail (rail maintenance)
19. Track Bonding
20. Station Maintenance

The maintenance costs associated with power distribution systems are commonly included under a set of accounts separate from the rest of the way-and-structures accounts.

Power Supply and Distribution

21. Signal System (other than way section portion)
22. Communication System
23. Supervisory Control Equipment
24. Underground Conduits
25. Feeders—Overhead and Underground
26. Third-Rail Electrical Maintenance
27. Miscellaneous Electric Line Expenses
28. Emergency Crews

Track maintenance costs (that is, roughly those included in the first eight preceding accounts) constitute the largest share of total way-and-structures expense. These costs are primarily a function of the annual gross tonnage of equipment passing over a track. The remaining costs are largely a function of track miles (that is, the size of the property), though it would be reasonable to expect some economies of scale in this respect.

Table 6.1 shows annual cost of maintenance of way and structures, estimated annual gross tonnage, and track mileage for five operating properties. The variation in the resulting unit costs per ton-mile and per track-mile is probably due to the different characteristics of the properties involved. In Cleveland, for example, the facilities are relatively new and most of the track is located in open cut where maintenance costs are generally less than for underground or elevated track. In Philadelphia, on the other hand, much of the track is located on old elevated structures where one would expect maintenance of way and structures to be more costly. Other differences between properties, such as curvature (which tends to increase track maintenance costs), acceleration and braking rates, and the number of "wheel passes," may account for some of the variation in maintenance-of-way costs. In Toronto, for example, the number of wheel passes (that is, car-miles per mile) is very high although facilities are new, while in Chicago the high

Table 6.1. Maintenance-of-Way Costs—1960

Property	Cleveland	Toronto	Philadelphia[†]	Chicago	New York
Annual Revenue (In car-miles)	7,703,000	7,053,000	10,200,000	44,633,000	305,570,000
Revenue Track-Miles	29.8	8.82	26.0	160.7	723.4
Annual Car-Miles per Revenue Track-Mile	158,000	800,000	392,000	278,000	422,000
Approximate Car Weight (In pounds)*	65,000	96,000	59,000	53,000	92,000
Annual Ton-Miles per Revenue Track-Mile	5.1×10^6	38.4×10^6	11.6×10^6	7.4×10^6	19.4×10^6
Total Annual M-of-W Cost	$266,000	$1,060,000	$1,100,000	$3,678,000	$40,211,000
Unit Annual M-of-W Costs: Dollars per TGTM per Mile[‡]	1.75	3.13	3.65	3.09	2.86
Dollars per Track-Mile	8900	120,200	42,300	22,900	55,600
Cents per Car-Mile	5.7	15.0	10.8	8.2	13.2

*Using a 40 per cent load factor applied to maximum rated car capacity and assuming an average passenger weight of 150 pounds.

[†]Due to a change in equipment used on this line during 1960, Philadelphia figures quoted in this and in following tables are based on a projection of the first seven months in 1961.

[‡]TGTM = thousand gross ton-miles.

maintenance costs may be attributed to extreme curvature. Cleveland, at the other extreme, has very little track curvature and relatively few wheel passes. These differences, however, do not entirely explain away the variation among properties. The ultimate explanation may be simply that the available data constitute too small a sample.

6.3 Maintenance of Equipment

Maintenance-of-equipment costs are those associated with the repair and upkeep of the vehicles on a rail transit system. They comprise from 10 to 15 per cent of total operating and maintenance costs. The following representative set of accounts suggests more precisely the items included in this general cost category:

1. Maintenance of Passenger Car Bodies
2. Painting Passenger Cars
3. Maintenance of Passenger Car Trucks
4. Accident Repairs
5. Maintenance of Rail Service Cars
6. Electric Motive Equipment, Passenger Cars
7. Electric Motive Equipment, Rail Service Cars
8. Shop Expenses
9. Car Cleaning, Oiling, and Inspection
10. Miscellaneous Car Service
11. Maintenance of Fare Collection Equipment

Maintenance-of-equipment costs vary largely with equipment utilization, that is, with car-hours of operation. This accounts

for some of the variation in per-car-mile maintenance costs shown
in Table 6.2 (where costs are listed for the same operating companies shown in Table 6.1). In Cleveland, for example, where average car speeds are much higher than for either of the other two

Table 6.2. Maintenance-of-Equipment Costs—1960

Property	Cleveland	Toronto	Philadelphia	Chicago	New York
Total Annual Maintenance of Equipment Costs*	194,000	602,000‡	700,000	4,431,000	29,984,000**
Cents per Car-Mile	4.1	8.5	6.9	9.9	9.8
Average Car Speed (In miles per hour)	28.9	16.0	21.0	22.0	18.0
Car Length (In feet)	48	57	55	48	51-60
Car-Miles per Car	53,400	50,700	37,800	40,200	46,500
Car Weight (In 1000 pounds)	57	84	59	44	74-84
Total Number of Cars	88	140	270	1110	6565
Average Car-Age (In years)	6	6	1	19	23
Dollars per Car-Hour	1.18	1.36	1.45	2.17	1.82

*Accounting procedures are not entirely standard from one property to another. Some prop-
erties, for example, include the cost of car cleaning under equipment maintenance while others
include this cost under transportation. Car hostling (the forming or breaking up of trains) is
also charged to one or the other of these accounts. To account for these differences the authors
have included car servicing costs under equipment maintenance, and car hostling costs under
transportation. The available cost data have therefore been adjusted to make accounts comparable as follows:

  †Includes $2,700 for car servicing deducted from Table 6.3.

  ‡Excluded approximately $324,000 for car hostling added to Table 6.3.

  **Includes $2,797,000 for car servicing deducted from Table 6.3.

properties using new equipment, equipment maintenance costs are
substantially lower. Moreover for the three companies using new
equipment (Cleveland, Toronto, and Philadelphia), maintenance
costs per car-hour are seen to decrease with increasing car-
mileage, which suggests there are economies of scale to be obtained with higher utilization.

6.4 Conducting Transportation

This category includes all the costs of conducting transportation
except the cost of electric power. That is, it includes all the costs
of operating a transit system given the necessary fixed facilities,
equipment, and power. The following representative set of accounts includes figures to show an approximate breakdown of the
various costs within this general category:

	Approximate Percentage of Total Transportation Costs
1. Motormen[4]	15-20
2. Guards	15-20
3. Yardmen and Switchmen	5-15
4. Platform Men	0-4
5. Station Collectors	20-25
6. Operation of Signals and Interlocking Systems	5-10
7. Other Transportation Expenses	0-2
8. Other Station Expenses	5-10
9. Superintendence	5-10
10. Operation of Telephone Systems	—
11. Clearing Wrecks	—

On most properties, conducting transportation accounts for approximately 50 per cent of the total cost of maintenance and operation. As just shown, the wages of motormen, guards, and station personnel in turn account for the majority of the cost of conducting transportation. The circumstances of their employment are therefore of interest in understanding the structure of rail transit costs.

As discussed in Chapter 7, the demand for rail transit service is concentrated largely in the 3 or 4 morning and evening rush hours of each weekday. The demand for train service and station personnel obviously follows this same pattern. In the early days of transit it was possible to employ labor for these rush hours only, allowing them to engage in whatever other employment they wanted during the midday hours. This practice had obvious disadvantages from the employee's standpoint. Today, union agreements severely limit the use of such "swing shifts," and those that are permitted for train service personnel may not extend over a total spread of more than $10\frac{1}{2}$ hours without the payment of overtime. In addition, all employees must be guaranteed a minimum work week.

Other contract provisions increase the hours of overtime pay even when total work hours for the week are less than the straight time limit. These include time allowances for reporting in and out, resting between runs, ferrying between runs, and so forth. Legal regulations may also contribute to a high level of labor costs. In Boston, for instance, the law requires a guard between

---

[4] Includes allowances for traveling, extras, spread of hours, guarantees, Sunday time, overtime, delay time, and ferrying time.

every pair of cars to operate the doors.   Under this law ten-car
trains would require five guards, though other cities successful-
ly operate such trains with one.

The predictable result of such restrictions is that rail transit
systems incur high labor costs for relatively few man-hours of
work.   The large labor force employed for the morning and evening rush must work well below capacity during the rest of the
day and is not permitted to engage in other than operating duties.

Table 6.3 shows the per-car-mile cost of conducting transportation on five different transit properties.   The general agreement

Table 6.3. Costs of Conducting Transportation—1960

Property	Cleveland	Toronto	Philadelphia	Chicago	New York
Total Annual Trans- portation Costs*	1,182,000	1,280,000	3,150,000	13,313,000	81,182,000
Transportation Costs (In cents per car- mile)	25.1	18.1	30.9	29.8	26.5

*Adjusted to make accounts comparable as follows:

Cleveland: excludes $2,700 for car servicing added to Table 6.2.

Toronto: includes approximately $324,000 for car hostling deducted from Table 6.2.

New York: excludes $2,797,000 for car servicing added to Table 6.2.

among these costs is fair.   The markedly lower cost for Toronto
is actually no exception, since it can be attributed almost entirely to the higher car mileage that results from running maximum
length trains throughout the day on that property.   (It is common
practice elsewhere to reduce the length of trains during off-peak
hours.)[5]

6.5 Power Costs

This category includes all those costs associated with the purchase (or production), transmission, and distribution of electrical

---

[5] The authors made paper redispatches for the Toronto operation using shorter trains during off-peak hours. This produced
theoretical savings in total car-miles of from 19 to 25 per cent.
Assuming the total cost of labor for conducting transportation did
not change, this adjustment in car-mileage would raise the unit
costs to about 22 cents per car-mile. In addition, hourly wage
rates in Toronto tend to be lower than in the U. S. cities considered here. (If shorter trains were actually used in this fashion,
there would be some increase in the cost of switching and hostling
equipment. This would show up in the cost of conducting transportation on a car-mile basis. Presumably there would also be
some reduction in the total cost of car maintenance, though this
should not have any significant effect on unit costs per car-mile.)

energy to the rail transit vehicle. (Maintenance of power supply and distribution systems is included under maintenance of way
and structures.) The following accounts are generally included in
this category:

1. Electrical Maintenance of Substations
2. Substation Employees
3. Supervisory Control Operation
4. Substation Supplies and Expenses
5. Equipment Maintenance
6. Transmission System Maintenance
7. Power Purchases

In the past it was common for large transit properties operating
electric vehicles to produce their own power and in many cases to
supplement transit revenues by the sale of surplus power. Because
of their poor load factor (high demand for short periods), however,
it has become difficult for transit operators to produce power at a
cost lower than it can be purchased commercially. Thus, in recent years many transit properties have sold their power-produc-
ing facilities, electing instead to rely on the purchase of electric
power from public utilities.

Power consumption depends upon a number of factors. These
include car weight, horsepower/weight ratio, acceleration rates,
maximum running speed, alignment characteristics such as gradient and curvature, and frequency of station stops.

The weight factor drops out when one considers power consumption on a ton-mile basis. Of the remaining factors station frequency and power/weight ratio are probably the most important.
Since energy requirements are higher during periods of acceleration than while moving at constant speeds, power consumption increases with increasing station frequency. Power/weight ratio is
important through its effect on acceleration. An increased power/
weight ratio makes it possible to reach maximum running speed in
a shorter time. Additional energy is thus required to travel at
high constant speed during the time saved.

Power costs depend not only upon power consumption but also
on kilowatt-hour rates. These rates are in turn dependent partly
upon total consumption, but more importantly upon the peak rate
of consumption. Unfortunately, the peak demand for transit power
coincides roughly with the peak demand of other commercial power users. Thus, transit companies generally pay a high average
kilowatt-hour rate for their power, though actual rates vary widely from one property to the next.

Table 6.4 shows unit power consumption as well as power costs
on both a car-mile and ton-mile basis. The differences in power
costs on a car-mile basis can be partly explained by the large differences in kilowatt-hour rates, but it is more difficult to account
for the variation in power consumption per ton-mile. The higher

Table 6.4. Power Costs—1960

Property	Cleveland	Toronto	Philadelphia	Chicago	New York
Annual Car-Miles (In 1000's)	4,703	7,053	10,200	44,633	305,570
Approximate Car Weight (In tons—loaded)	33	48	30	27	46
Total Horsepower	220	260	400	220	400
Horsepower per Ton	6.7	5.4	13.6	8.1	8.7
Total Annual Power Cost	207,000	596,000	930,000	4,356,000	34,628,000
Average Power Cost: Cents per Car-Mile	4.4	8.5	9.1	9.8	11.3
Cents per Ton-Mile	.133	.177	.308	.362	.245
Kilowatt-hour Rate (In cents)	1.072	0.57	1.54	1.876	2.22
Annual Power Consumption (In Kilowatt-hours $\times 10^3$)	17,000	36,000	60,000	203,000	1,660,000
Average Power Consumption (In Kilowatt-hours per car-mile)	3.6	5.2	5.9	4.5	5.4
Kilowatt-Hours per Ton-Mile	.109	.108	.200	.166	.118

power requirements of Chicago and Philadelphia over Cleveland,
for example, could be largely a function of station frequency. As
station frequency increases in moving from Cleveland to Chicago
and Philadelphia, power consumption per ton-mile also increases.
The high power/weight ratio of the Philadelphia cars also helps
account for the higher energy requirements of that system.

6.6 Other Operating Expenses

A number of miscellaneous cost items do not fall clearly under
any of the four general headings already discussed. These include
such costs as administration, stationery and printing, insurance,
injuries, damages, materials handling, and sales expense. Unfortunately, there is little or no uniformity among the various operating companies in accounting for these costs. Many companies,
moreover, do not differentiate between their rail transit and surface operations in reporting on such costs. This makes generalizations about them difficult.

The costs in this category probably depend largely on the size
of the operation. This suggests that they might best be estimated
as some fixed percentage of all other operating and maintenance
costs. (One might expect some economies of scale in these costs,
but the data do not seem to substantiate that hypothesis.) Table
6.5 shows estimates of these costs for the five operating companies previously discussed.

6.7   Total Operating and Maintenance Costs

The results of Tables 6.1 through 6.5 are summarized in Table 6.6. It should be noted again that car-miles, though they are probably the best single production index on which to base costs, are

Table 6.5. Other Operating Expenses—1960

Property	Cleveland	Toronto	Philadelphia	Chicago	New York
Basic Operating and Maintenance Expense (In $1000)*	1,849	3,538	6,280	25,778	186,005
Other Operating Expenses (In $1000)†	295	371	900	4,039	27,519
Total Operating and Maintenance Expenses (In $1000)	2,144	3,909	7,180	29,817	213,524
Other Expenses as a Percentage of Basic Expenses	16.0	10.5	14.3	15.7	14.8
Other Expenses (In cents per car-mile)	6.3	5.3	8.8	9.0	9.0

*Includes maintenance-of-way, maintenance-of-equipment, conducting-transportation, and power costs.
†The Toronto figures represent estimates prorated from system totals (including bus, trolley coach, and streetcar operations).

Table 6.6. Total Operating and Maintenance Costs Cents per Car-Mile—1960

Property	Cleveland	Toronto	Philadelphia	Chicago	New York
Maintenance of Way	5.7	15.0	10.8	8.2	13.2
Maintenance of Equipment	4.1	8.5	6.9	9.9	9.8
Conducting Transportation	25.1	18.1	30.9	29.8	26.5
Power	4.4	8.5	9.1	9.8	11.3
Other Operating	6.3	5.3	8.8	9.0	9.0
Total Operating and Maintenance	45.6	55.4	66.5	66.7	69.8

not entirely satisfactory in this regard. In particular, way-and-structures costs and power costs do not correlate well with car-miles.

It is also of interest to know the approximate percentage of total costs which fall in each of these five major cost categories and the proportion of each which can be attributed to labor. In general, the

unit costs of labor can be expected to increase faster than costs
such as those for materials and power. Labor cost is therefore
important in comparing cost trends in rail transit with those for
competing forms of transportation. This information is also helpful in identifying those aspects of rail transit operation wherein
significant cost reductions may be possible.

Table 6.7 shows estimated averages for the percentages of total
costs and of labor in each major cost category. These should be
considered only approximations, inasmuch as the actual figures
vary somewhat among the operating companies studied.

Table 6.7. Breakdown of Total Operating and Maintenance
Costs and Per Cent of Labor
(Five Properties—1960)

	Percentage of Total	Percentage Labor	Labor as Percentage of Total
Way and Structures	15	79	12
Maintenance of Equipment	14	74	10
Conducting Transportation	44	97	43
Power	15	17	3
Other Operating Expenses	12	22	3
Totals	100%		71%

6.8 Costs and Rush-Hour Capacity

The planner and the design engineer are particularly interested
in the ability of rail transit to carry large numbers of rush-hour
(peak-hour) passengers at cost and service levels that are competitive with other forms of urban transportation. These three measures of performance—rush-hour capacity, unit costs, and quality
of service—are closely interrelated. Given a particular level of
rush-hour demand, the desired quality of service (in terms of car
floor space per passenger) determines the requirements for system rush-hour capacity. Rush-hour capacity largely determines
total equipment requirements, manpower requirements, and peak
power demand. These in turn largely determine the total costs of
operation, and, because the level of off-peak service provided generally follows from that in the rush hours, the unit costs as well.
The essential task of this chapter is to trace this relationship between unit costs, service quality, and peak-hour capacity.

It should be remembered that both unit costs (to the extent they
are reflected in fare levels) and service quality have a major

effect upon transit demand. Thus, the chain of cause and effect actually comes full circle. For purposes of analysis it is convenient to cut into this circle as we have here, considering first the cost and service capabilities of a system, given a certain demand to meet (and thus a certain capacity to provide), and then considering, as we will in the next chapter, the effect of these manifested capabilities upon demand.

The fundamental measure of capacity in which we are interested is the number of passengers carried per hour past a given point. In determining costs, however, it is more convenient to state capacity in terms of square feet of usable car floor area passing per hour. Multiplying this figure by a passenger-loading coefficient (such as discussed in Chapter 4) will in turn yield passengers per hour. The loading coefficient itself is one of the two most important measures of service quality, and stating capacity in this way allows us to take it into account.

The other important measure of service quality is average running speed. This is determined largely by horsepower/weight ratios and average station spacing. Its most important effect on costs is as a determinant of equipment and train labor requirements. It also affects power costs, though to a lesser extent. Fortunately, the complex relationship between running speed and track capacity (see Chapter 5) can be overlooked in the present analysis, as it is of interest only in very high capacity operations.

The relationships between equipment characteristics and cost can also be important. As just pointed out horsepower/weight ratio affects speed and thus costs. Car weight per square foot of floor area affects both maintenance-of-equipment cost and the cost of conducting transportation. Finally, the initial cost (per square foot of floor area) of equipment is obviously a major determinant of total unit costs.

The graphs on the following pages reflect the more important of these relationships in summary form. Appendix B explains the development of these graphs from the empirical cost information presented previously. It is important to bear in mind the shortcomings of this cost information as explained earlier. Certainly the absolute value of the unit costs shown on these graphs must be used with caution. At best these costs only reflect average conditions, and no single transit operation can ever be "average." The principal function of these graphs, in any case, is to identify the way in which changes in the various characteristics of a system can affect its costs. For these purposes, relative costs interest us more than absolute costs.

Figure 6.1 shows the cost relationships most important to our general discussion: the effect of rush-hour capacity (in one-way square-foot miles per hour per mile of route) upon each of the three major cost categories—the carrying costs of permanent way and structures, the carrying costs of equipment, and the costs of operation and maintenance. Figure 6.2 shows the same information in the form of total unit costs.

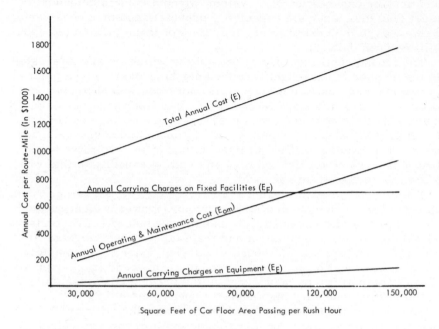

Figure 6.1. Annual route-mile costs (for assumed conditions outlined in Appendix B, Section 3).

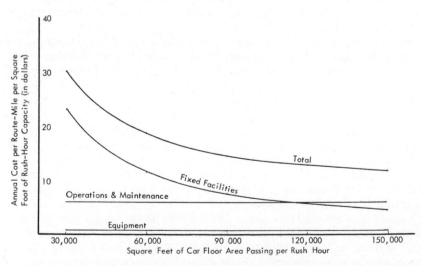

Figure 6.2. Annual route-mile costs per unit of rush-hour capacity (for assumed conditions outlined in Appendix B, Section 3).

The cost relationships shown in these figures are based upon the
sample cost computation in Appendix B and incorporate the assumptions as to car size and weight, average speed, and average cost
figures cited there. (See pp. 131 through 135.) These assumptions affect absolute costs, but they do not affect the general form
of the indicated cost-capacity relationships. (One should note particularly, however, that a constant cost per mile for fixed facilities has been assumed throughout the entire range of capacities
shown. In practice these costs would increase somewhat with increasing capacity as explained in Appendix B, Section 2.)

Figure 6.2 shows clearly the decreasing unit costs that can be obtained in high-capacity operation as a result of the spreading of
fixed costs. It also reveals the overwhelming importance that the
cost of fixed facilities may assume. The sample computation upon
which these curves are based assumes a construction cost of
$15,000,000 per mile for fixed facilities, which is reasonably rep-
resentative of subway construction in built-up urban areas.

In Figure 6.3, a family of curves shows the variation of total passenger-mile costs with rush-hour capacity for different route-mile

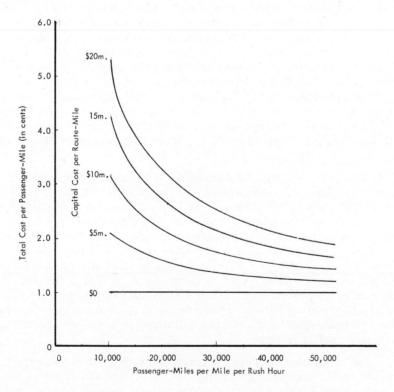

Figure 6.3. Passenger-mile costs versus rush-hour capacity
(for assumed conditions outlined in Appendix B, Section 3).

construction costs. These curves have also been computed on the basis of the assumed conditions outlined in Appendix B. Similar curves can be obtained for any other combination of first cost, capital recovery factor, equipment cost and performance characteristics, station costs, and unit operating costs. For any particular route-mile construction cost, increasing station spacing will also generally imply moving down to a lower construction cost with a corresponding decrease in total unit costs. (As suggested by Table 3.3, this decrease in route-mile construction cost might range from $160,000 to $2.5 million per station per mile.)

Notice that with zero construction costs (that is, where the cost of fixed facilities can be disregarded for one reason or another) the total unit costs are constant and independent of capacity. Although economies of scale might be expected with increased output, they are not reflected here, because we are using average rather than incremental costs.

Perhaps the most critical factor in computing cost relationships such as those shown in Figure 6.3 is the interest rate used in converting capital costs to annual costs. For fully self-supporting systems the proper interest rate is probably that at which money for capital expenditures can be borrowed.[6] (An interest rate of 4 per cent was chosen on this basis for the sample computations in Appendix B.) For systems whose capital expenditures are subsidized out of general tax receipts, the choice of a proper interest rate is less straightforward. In theory this rate should reflect the potential return on other (public) investment opportunities foregone; that is, it should be equal to the "opportunity cost" of capital.[7] Since these opportunities may include such things as schools, the "return" on which is not easy to express in money terms, this cost is difficult to determine. Professor E. L. Grant has suggested that a rate

---

[6] This interest rate will be somewhat lower for publicly owned systems than for those that are privately owned. Proponents of public rather than private ownership use this fact in arguing their case. One should not ignore, however, the adverse effect that issuance of bonds for transit financing may have upon the ability of a government to borrow money for other public works.

[7] Proposed Practices for Economic Analysis of River Basin Projects, Report to the Inter-Agency Committee on Water Resources by the Subcommittee on Evaluation Standards, Washington D. C., Government Printing Office, 1958, or as it is commonly referred to, the "Green-Book" includes the following in a discussion of the opportunity cost of money:

. . . the minimum interest rate appropriate for use in project evaluation for converting estimates of benefits and costs to a common time basis is the risk-free return expected to be realized on capital invested in alternative uses.

of at least 7 per cent should be used for highways.[8]   If you consider the somewhat greater difficulties associated with financing transit investments, even this rate may be too low.

To illustrate the importance of the interest rate, it is useful to
recompute some of the points on the curves of Figure 6.3 at 6 per
cent rather than 4 per cent. Table 6.8 compares the results of
such a recomputation. The table shows clearly that an increase in
interest rate can be especially significant for high-capital-cost
systems operating at low capacity.

Table 6.8. The Effect of Interest Rate on Total Unit Costs*

	10,500 Passengers per Rush Hour		30,500 Passengers per Rush Hour	
Interest Rate	i = 4%	i = 6%	i = 4%	i = 6%
Construction Cost:				
$5,000,000 per Mile	2.1	2.5	1.4	1.5
$15,000,000 per Mile	4.3	5.5	2.1	2.5

*All unit costs in cents per passenger-mile. Unit costs for
i = 4 per cent taken directly from curves in Figure 6.3.

6.9 The Effect of Service Quality

As was pointed out in the previous section, both cost and capacity
are also closely related to certain aspects of service quality. Figure 6.3, for instance, could be modified to show the cost savings
that would result from an increase in station spacing. This sort of
change would affect service quality in two ways. It would increase
average running speed, an improvement in service quality. At the
same time, it would make passenger access to the transit system
less convenient and thus be a detriment to service quality. The net
effect of these conflicting effects is difficult to determine even when
confronted with all the facts of a specific case.

A more obvious measure of service quality is the passenger-
loading coefficient. Figure 6.4 shows its effect on both cost and capacity, again for the assumed conditions outlined in the sample
computation of Appendix B, Section 3. As mentioned in Section 4.5
of Chapter 4, a loading coefficient of 0.15 passenger per square
foot is approximately that required to give everyone a seat, a level
of service often demanded in verbal battles over transit. A loading

---

[8] See Eugene L. Grant, "Interest and the Rate of Return on Invest-
ment," Economic Analysis in Highway Programming, Location and
Design, Highway Research Board Special Report 56, Washington
D. C., 1960, pp. 82-90.

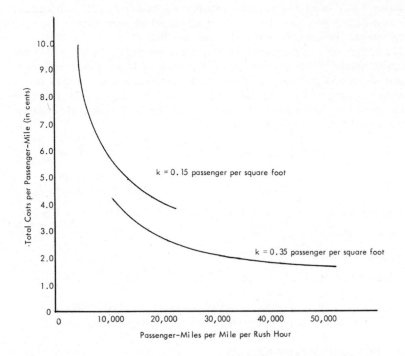

Figure 6.4. The effect of loading coefficient on passenger-mile costs (for assumed conditions outlined in Appendix B, Section 3).

coefficient of 0.35 provides for a substantial proportion of standees, but it is by no means the ultimate in crowding experienced on existing transit operations during rush hours.

With the two-minute headways and ten-car trains used in this example, a loading coefficient of 0.15 limits maximum capacity to 22,500 passengers per hour. A loading coefficient of 0.35 permits an increase in this capacity limit to 52,500 passengers per hour.

The effect of a higher loading coefficient on costs is equally significant. For a capacity of 20,000 passengers per hour, the higher loading coefficient results in a 30 per cent reduction in unit costs. From the standpoint of the planner and engineer the difficulty lies in comparing this saving in money cost to the penalty that an average passenger attaches to the less comfortable circumstances in which he must ride.

Chapter 7

RAIL TRANSIT AND THE DEMAND
FOR URBAN TRANSPORTATION

The character and magnitude of the demand for transit transportation are the most important factors to be considered in the planning and design of a rail transit system. They determine whether transit service should be provided at all and, if so, where lines should be located. They form the basis for detailed decisions on such matters as station size and spacing, equipment requirements, signal system design, and trackage layouts. They not only affect costs (as shown in Chapter 6), but they also determine revenues; that is, they control the financial destiny of any system, present or future.

Yet, for all this, transit planners and engineers have often paid little attention to the problem of forecasting demand. This tendency to overlook so important a problem results partly from real or imagined limits on the capital available for the design of a project. Building even the simplest transit facility and running even a single train requires a costly engineering effort. A thorough demand study has virtually no effect upon reaching this tangible goal. The need for a careful demand forecast can thus be ignored all too easily when capital funds are allocated.

The general failure to study demand also results from a simple lack of knowledge on the subject. At best the demand for any type of passenger transportation is an extremely complex phenomenon and one subject to great uncertainty. The demand for urban transit depends in an intimate way not only upon the market that it serves, but also upon the highway facilities with which it must compete. The demand for a transit system that will reach physical maturity in 15 or 20 years, moreover, depends upon a future market and a future set of competing transportation systems the character of which is extremely difficult to predict. The limited methodological capabilities of traditional planning and engineering have simply been unequal to this complexity. Fortunately, these methodological deficiencies are gradually being overcome.

Notwithstanding this question of methodological shortcomings, there is much about the demand for transit that the characteristics of past and present usage can help explain. There is also much that the relative cost and service characteristics of rail transit

and its automobile and bus competitors can tell us. A discussion
of these two subjects can therefore put the problem of estimating
transit demand in better perspective.

7.1 The Characteristics of Rail Transit Usage

As discussed in Chapter 1,[1] the available figures on transit usage
indicate a general decline in riding which has become particularly
noticeable since the end of World War II.[2] The New York City
Transit Authority has pointed out what are probably the major reasons for this trend.

> The 5-day week, population shifts, increased availability and
> use of private cars, television, relocation of shopping centers,
> changing business conditions and altered patterns of vacation
> and recreation activities have all been recognized as contribu-
> ting factors to the general trend against mass transit use.

More subtle but in some ways more serious than the general decline in total riding has been the decline in the proportion of off-
peak to total riding. The effect of this has been to hold the level of
total operating costs up, even though the total traffic base has been
steadily shrinking. Tables 7.1 and 7.2 point up this shift in the
character of transit demand.

Table 7.1. Peak-Hour Rail Transit Passengers as a Percentage of Total Weekday Patronage (Chicago)*

Year	Percentage Carried during 4 Peak Hours
1955	55.2
1956	55.7
1957	56.1
1958	56.6
1959	57.0
1960	57.5
1961	57.9

*Data transmitted in a letter from C. B. North, Chicago Transit
Authority, March 29, 1962, to R. M. Soberman.

Figure 7.1 demonstrates this problem graphically. Only commuter railroads (whose market orientation has the same general
characteristics as that of rail transit) have fared so badly with respect to off-peak patronage.

[1] See Figure 1.1.
[2] New York City Transit Authority (NYCTA), Annual Report for
the Year Ended June 30, 1960, New York, 1960, p. 8.

Table 7.2. Weekend and Holiday Transit Passengers
as a Percentage of Weekday Passengers
(New York)*

Year	Per Cent
1956	38.6
1957	39.0
1958	37.2
1959	38.2
1960	37.3

*NYCTA, Annual Report 1960, p. 12.

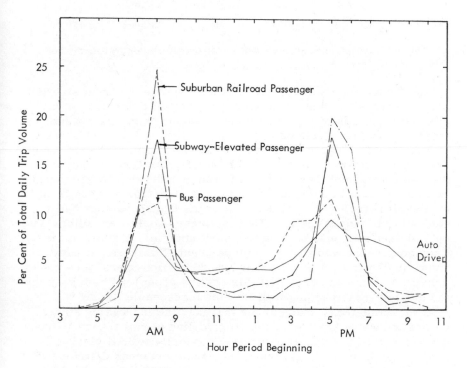

Figure 7.1. Hourly percentages of total daily trip volume of
each mode of travel.
Source: Chicago Area Transportation Study, Final Report,
Vol. 1, Chicago, 1959, p. 48.

More recently, however there have been some indications that
the decline in total patronage may be "bottoming out." Many transit operators feel that the future trend will be up, not down. Table
7.3 suggests this may be true in some cases.

Table 7.3. Recent Trends in Rail Transit Patronage
(Passengers carried in 1000's)

Year	New York	Cleveland	Chicago	Toronto	Philadelphia[*]
1955	1,378,000	8,100	112,900	35,100	149,900
1956	1,363,000	14,700	115,700	36,200	146,000
1957	1,355,000	15,700	112,300	36,600	139,700
1958	1,319,000	15,500	107,100	35,900	134,100
1959	1,324,000	17,800	113,300	35,900	130,700
1960	1,345,000	18,300	112,900	34,700	131,600
1961	1,363,000	17,800	110,100	33,000	135,400

[*]Includes transfer passengers that are approximately equal in number
to ticket passengers.

One can advance several explanations for this apparent stabili-
zation in transit riding. One theory is that all those people with
alternative means of travel have now stopped using transit and
that the remainder have no choice but to stay with it. This class
of rider is thus "captive" to public transportation. Many of these
are school children. Many are old or infirm. Many simply do
not own an automobile. A study of transit ridership in Pittsburgh
(where, it should be noted, there is only streetcar and bus transit
available) revealed that 85 per cent of the transit patrons had no
choice but to ride transit.[3]   That is, these people were either without a driver's license or without an automobile. A study in the
Chicago area showed that over 50 per cent of rail transit users
and over 65 per cent of all public transportation users were non-
drivers.[4]   One can argue that this captive group will help keep up
the level of transit riding well into the foreseeable future.

At the same time, many argue that it is the increasing street
congestion which has halted the long decline of rail transit patronage and will soon force it up again. Certainly transit plays a
strong role in trips to and from the central business district (CBD),
where traffic congestion is often greatest. In Chicago, for instance,
rail transportation (transit and commuter railroad) accounts for
approximately 45 per cent of all the person-trips made to the CBD,
though it handles only 15 per cent of the total person-trips throughout

[3] Louis E. Keefer, "Choice Transit Trips," Pittsburgh Area
Transportation Study Research Letter, Vol. 3, No. 1, January-
February 1961, pp. 4-5.

[4] Illinois State Mass Transportation Commission, The Mass
Transportation Problem in Illinois, Chicago, 1959, pp. 38-40.

the entire metropolitan area.[5]   In New York City, rail transit alone
accounts for 60 per cent of the trips entering Manhattan south of
61st Street.[6] In Cleveland a survey of rail transit patrons boarding
outside the downtown area indicated that 35 per cent of them had
elected to park their automobiles and ride the transit downtown.[7]
Where rail as well as bus transit is available, moreover, the two
together apparently capture a larger share of downtown traffic than
bus transit can alone.   Table 7.4 shows this.

Table 7.4. Percentage of CBD Trips Carried by Public Transit[*]
(Selected cities)

City	Year	Urbanized Area Population—1950	Percentage of CBD Trips via Transit
New York	1956	12,296,000	77.8[†]
Chicago	1960	4,921,000	59.4[†]
Los Angeles	1960	3,997,000	24.8
Philadelphia	1955	2,922,000	52.7[†]
Boston	1954	2,233,000	58.2[†]
San Francisco	1954	2,022,000	49.0
St. Louis	1957	1,400,000	28.4
Cleveland	1954	1,384,000	54.0[†]
Toronto	1955	1,253,000	57.6[†]
Baltimore	1955	1,162,000	31.0
Milwaukee	1958	829,000	32.4

[*]Wilbur Smith and Associates, Future Highways and Urban
Growth, New Haven, 1961, p. 100.
[†]Rail Transit Available.

Whether or not the combination of captive riders and the com-
pounding of urban street congestion will produce a resurgence in
transit revenues remains to be seen. As Table 7.5 suggests, the
picture is less promising when viewed from the standpoint of rides
per capita, that is, "riding habit." In this respect at least, rail
transit hardly seems a "growth" industry.

---

[5] Chicago Area Transportation Study, Final Report, Vol. 1, Chicago, 1959, pp. 41, 47.
[6] Regional Plan Association, Hub-Bound Travel, New York,
1959, p. 4.
[7] Results of a postcard survey taken May 19, 1959, at West Park
and Triskett Rapid Transit Stations. (Source: Cleveland Transit
System.)

Table 7.5. Riding Habit
(Annual round-trip transit rides per capita)

Year	Chicago*	New York
1947	—	265
1950	—	213
1956	32	169
1960	32	—

*Based on population figures given in Chicago Area Transportation Study, Final Report, Vol. 2, p. 116, and transit-riding figures of Table 7.3.

New York City Transit Authority, Annual Report, 1960.

7.2 Rail Transit in the Transportation Market

Transportation systems, modes, or routes compete as sellers in the travel market on the basis of both cost and service. The traveler who as a buyer makes a choice in this market actually sees cost and service in the same light. On any given trip a traveler incurs a certain (1) money cost, (2) time loss, (3) discomfort, (4) inconvenience in making terminal connections and transfers, (5) uncertainty regarding time of arrival, and (6) possibility of accident. Though the last five of these usually come under the heading of "service factors," from the traveler's point of view they are all costs. The relative importance that each traveler attaches to these six "cost" factors effectively determines his choice of transportation. Different travelers will, of course, make different value judgments about these factors (judgments which in turn depend upon other factors such as income level and car ownership), but their collective judgment constitutes the basis for transportation demand.

An evaluation of rail transit relative to either its present or its future competitors must thus be set in the context of these costs and service characteristics as the traveler sees them. The ultimate test of a transportation system lies not in any technoeconomic indices of efficiency but in the extent to which it finds acceptance within the total value scheme of the community it serves.

An analysis of the relative cost and service capabilities of competing modes of urban transportation presents many difficulties. Rail transit costs, for instance, will vary widely, depending upon construction costs and peak-hour patronage in particular. (Figure 6.3 has shown this.) Trip length affects the money cost per passenger-mile when travelers pay the flat fares which are usual for most transit operations on this continent. The question of marginal versus full costs introduces a special complication in evaluating automobile transportation. Parking charges introduce another. In spite of these difficulties, we can still make some generalizations about money costs that help explain the relative position of automobiles, buses, and rail transit, the three major competitors in the urban transportation market.

We can say much less about service quality, despite its being equally if not more important than money costs. The difficulties here stem from three sources. The first is the extreme variability of the values that travelers attach to different levels of service quality. A second source of difficulty lies in the typical traveler's lack of adequate or accurate information on the actual physical characteristics of the alternative levels of service available to him. This distorts his reactions to the transportation market in ways that are difficult for the planner or engineer to predict, let alone state in any general terms. A third source of difficulty is our relative inability to transform service quality characteristics into value scales that are operationally satisfactory. That is, we cannot determine with any degree of satisfaction the money equivalent of a unit of trip time for even one class of travelers and one class of trips.

The economist would sum up all of these difficulties by saying that we know too little about the "demand functions" for urban passenger transportation. That is, even though we may be able to generalize about the performance range of alternative modes of transportation, we cannot make any generally satisfactory quantitative predictions about the way in which the market (urban travelers) will respond to this performance. In the context of the present discussion, this leaves us no choice but to make our comparison on a qualitative basis.

This does not preclude looking first at what we do know in a quantitative way about the various money costs involved. Figures 7.2 through 7.4 summarize these costs in graphical form as a function of trip length. (The source of these data and the major assumptions upon which they are based are given in the footnote below.) [8]

---

[8] The rail transit trip cost range has been shown in Figure 7.2 as from 3 to 6 cents per passenger-mile. The lower "limit" is based upon a rush-hour capacity of 40,000 persons per hour on a system costing $15 million per mile to construct. The resulting cost (see Figure 6.3) of 2 cents per passenger-mile was increased by 50 per cent to account for lighter rush-hour loadings at the extremities of the line. The upper "limit" is based upon a rush-hour capacity of 10,000 persons per hour and a construction cost of $15 million per mile. The resulting cost was similarly increased by 50 per cent.

The bus transit cost range has been shown as from 2 to 6 cents per passenger-mile. The lower limit is based upon a cost of 50 cents per bus-mile and an over-all daily average of 25 passengers per bus. The upper limit is based upon a cost of 75 cents per bus-mile and an over-all daily average of 12.5 passengers per bus.

The "connecting trip" cost shown as an increment on flat fare costs was computed on the assumption that the connection portion

(continued page 92)

Figure 7.2 shows rail transit costs as a band that reflects the general range over which they may vary. This band represents the cost of <u>providing</u> transportation. The actual money cost to the traveler may be quite different, especially where flat fares are in effect. We therefore also show the constant (flat-fare) trip costs for two different fare levels as well.

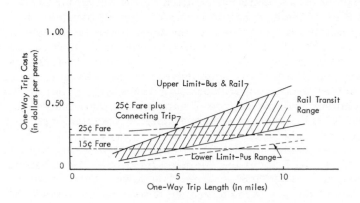

Figure 7.2. Transit trip costs.

The analysis in Chapter 6 serves as a basis for the rail transit costs shown here. No such analysis is available for bus transit. Estimates suggest, however, that the spread of passenger-mile costs for bus operation will be similar to, though on the whole lower than that for rail transit when the costs of fixed facilities are included. The figure shows some approximate limits for such costs. (One would have to question these closely in any <u>specific</u> situation.) of a transit trip was 24 per cent of the total trip length and would cost 5 cents per passenger-mile.

Automobile trip costs (Figure 7.3) have been computed on the assumption that automobile marginal operating costs were 4.5 cents per vehicle-mile and automobile full costs were 9.5 cents per vehicle-mile. For automobile costs, see Wilbur Smith and Associates, <u>Future Highways</u>, p. 149.

In combining costs (Figure 7.4) we have used 1.5 persons per auto as fairly representative of average conditions. We have also used a 20 cents flat transit fare in showing the effect of flat transit rates.

It should be noted that the schema here for representing the comparative money costs of urban trips are in no sense unique. Two important works in which similar comparisons appear are Wilfrid Owen, <u>The Metropolitan Transportation Problem</u>, Washington, D. C., 1956, p. 146; and Wilbur Smith and Associates, <u>Future Highways</u>, p. 151.

Again, while these suggested figures reflect the cost of providing transportation, a passenger paying on a flat-fare basis would find his per-mile costs somewhat different.

The connecting portions of a transit trip further complicate the identification of a traveler's money costs. On longer trips a traveler is likely to employ a subsidiary means of transportation to get to or from a transit system. This is the case with rail transit, where a traveler may use the bus, an automobile, or both to initiate or complete his trip. It is also true of bus transit where an automobile may be used. Figure 7.2 attempts to reflect this additional cost for one of the constant-fare lines.

Figure 7.3 shows the money costs of automobile trips under several conditions. The wide variation in these costs results from (1) the differing costs of parking at the away-from-home end of the trip, (2) whether or not the use of the car for the trips in question is what requires its ownership altogether, and (3) how many occupants there are in the vehicle.

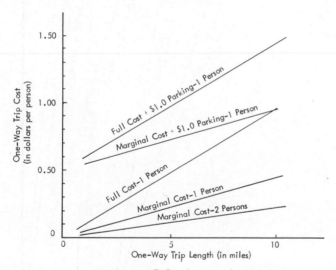

Figure 7.3. Auto trip costs.

Figure 7.4 permits a rough comparison of the money cost characteristics of all three modes, rail transit, bus transit, and automobile. More importantly, it helps summarize one dimension of the total picture of intermodal competition in the urban transportation market.

The total competitive picture is, of course, even more difficult to show. Any comparisons at this level are necessarily crude and can apply only to those parts of a metropolitan area where rail transit is readily available. Within these limitations, the attempt

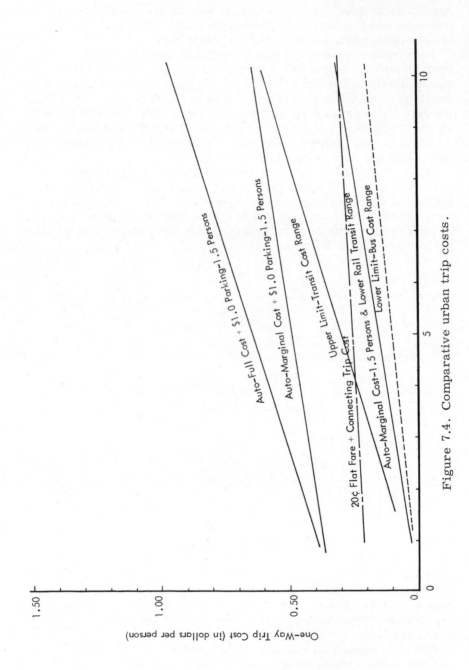

Figure 7.4. Comparative urban trip costs.

here (as summarized in Tables 7.6 and 7.7) is to reflect two somewhat different competitive situations: that which obtains during the
weekday rush hours and that which obtains during the off-peak hours
of the day (and week). The money costs incurred in consuming
transportation remain essentially constant from one time of day to
another (at least with current, admittedly less-than-rational pricing policies), but others among our total list of six cost dimensions
can change significantly.[9]   The following discussion will bring this
out.

Trip time is the second cost dimension considered in these tables.
General statements on the relative time costs for trips employing
different modes of transportation are difficult to make, because local conditions vary so widely in this respect. Some students of urban transportation problems have nonetheless been able to shed
light on this problem.[10]   Their findings suggest the following, very
approximate conclusions. During rush hours in densely built-up
metropolitan areas rail transit can match and often better the automobile in over-all trip time for those trips moving along the major
arteries of flow. Where the rail transit trip must connect with a
bus or automobile trip it is at less advantage. Our judgment (upon
which we are forced to rely for lack of any comprehensive data) is
that in the segment of the total rush-hour travel market which rail
transit potentially serves it offers trip times that are about equal
in the aggregate to those of the automobile.

The bus is in a less advantageous position. In general it can never equal over-all automobile time, even if it is operating largely
on a freeway. Cases where parking (or "unparking") an automobile is unusually time-consuming would be the only exception. All
things considered, bus trip times at rush hour probably are 50 per
cent to 100 per cent longer than those for automobiles. (This is
not meant to imply that certain express bus runs might not compare much better than that.)

Relative trip times are somewhat different during off-peak hours.
Several factors underlie this difference. The first is the obvious
factor of traffic congestion. Surface traffic generally moves with
much less delay during off-peak hours than it does during rush
hours. Whereas buses and automobiles may operate during rush

---

[9] The authors recognize that in the larger economic sense the
cost of providing off-peak transportation is less than that of providing rush-hour transportation. The discussion here is concerned
with the mechanism of the transportation market, however; and
that turns upon what the traveler pays, not upon the total commit-
ment of resources made by all sectors of the economy.

[10] See various data published by the American Transit Association. See also Francis Bello, "The City and the Car," Fortune,
October 1957, pp. 156ff; and especially Wilbur Smith and Associates, Future Highways, p. 150.

hours at a time cost disadvantage relative to grade-separated rail
transit, this disadvantage can disappear during the less crowded
off-peak hours.

The change from peak to off-peak hours in the geographical concentration of trip origins and destinations accentuates even further
this shift in relative trip time advantage. Peak hour trips are
largely work trips. Work trips tend to concentrate at one end in a
few geographical areas, preeminently the central business district.[11]
Off-peak-hour trips are made for a variety of purposes, and their
ends tend to be geographically dispersed. Transit routes, particularly rail transit routes, are laid out to serve usual trip patterns,
and these are work trips. Trips whose ends do not correspond with
these usual patterns will involve circuitous routing and often require connecting means of transportation if they are to be made by
transit. In general this means they will take more time.

A second-order effect is also at work on relative trip-time costs.
Because both rail and bus transit is in less demand during off-peak
hours, schedule frequency is usually reduced from rush-hour levels. This increases average passenger waiting time and thus over-
all trip-time costs.

The net effect, then, is to make transit and in particular rail
transit relatively more costly of the traveler's time in off-peak
hours. The distinction is particularly important, because travelers have come to attach such high value to their time that differences in time costs tend to outweigh other travel cost differences.
One should note, however, that different travelers still value their
time differently and also that any individual traveler may place different values upon his time depending upon the purpose of his trip.

A third dimension of urban travel costs is unreliability cost, that
is, the adverse or unwanted (from the traveler's point of view) con-
sequences associated with the failure of the transportation system
to deliver the traveler at his destination in the expected time. During rush hours rail transit generally has an edge on its competitors
in this regard. During off-peak hours this advantage may largely
disappear.

Discomfort is a cost dimension that may be of more importance.
Automobile travel is generally comfortable. Both bus and rail
transit are relatively uncomfortable. This difference is probably
greatest during the rush hours because of crowding in the buses
and trains. For many off-peak trips, moreover, travelers place
such a high premium on comfort that transit cannot compete in any
case. Our inclination is to feel that while rail transit may have a
slight advantage over buses, the automobile has a clear advantage
over both at all times of day.

Inconvenience is associated largely with public transit as contrasted to the private automobile. The need to wait at transit
stops, to transfer from one vehicle or mode of transportation to

---

[11] See the discussion in Chicago Area Transportation Study,
Final Report, Vol. 1, p. 43.

another, and generally to conform to the time constraints and geographical limitations of public transportation are all sources of inconvenience that the automobile avoids. Rail transit is at the greatest disadvantage in this respect. Bus transit falls somewhere between its two competitors. These differences in the extent of inconvenience are perhaps less important than trip-time costs, but may be equally as important as discomfort costs. Like time costs, moreover, the automobile's advantage in convenience is even more marked during off-peak hours.

The last of the six cost dimensions, accident cost, probably has relatively little effect upon the urban transportation market. To be sure, the accident costs associated with automobile transportation are demonstrably higher than those for either bus or rail transit. While this may be of some importance in a social welfare sense, it is difficult to believe that many travelers weigh this factor at all.

Table 7.6 summarizes these considerations for rush-hour travel. Remembering again that it applies only to those parts of an urban area in which rail and bus transit are practically available, this summary suggests two general conclusions. It suggests first that rail transit will often have a total rush-hour advantage over bus transit, primarily because of lower rush-hour trip times. It suggests further that while rail transit can have a total rush-hour advantage over automobile transportation, it can also be at a disadvantage. This issue turns largely upon the money and time costs of a rush-hour automobile trip. Where two or more persons can make the trip together, where parking costs are not high, or where only marginal automobile costs are chargeable to the trip, and where the time disadvantage of the automobile trip is not large when compared to rail transit, the automobile may be clearly preferable.

These conclusions conform well to the rush-hour travel market as we know it. The off-peak hour situation is different, however, both because traffic conditions on surface streets are different and because the character of trip demand is different. Table 7.7 shows the effect these changes have upon relative trip costs. Both rail and bus transit are somewhat more comfortable (i.e., have lower discomfort costs) in off-peak hours than in rush hours, but this factor is offset by the inconvenience of bus or rail transit for many off-peak hour trips. In the major category of trip time, moreover, rail transit suffers a serious competitive setback. While automobile trips speed up, transit trips slow down. The geographically less structured pattern of demand renders transit in general less direct and thus more time-consuming. Improved traffic conditions offset this somewhat for buses, but not for rail transit.

The change in off-peak demand affects relative money costs as well. Off-peak trips are generally shorter.[12] Automobile trips

_____

[12] See, for instance, Wilbur Smith and Associates, Future Highways, p. 105; or Chicago Area Transportation Study, Final Report, Vol. 1, p. 38.

Table 7.6. Relative Rush-Hour Trip Costs

Trip Costs	(Relative Importance)	Rail Transit	Bus Transit	Auto
Money		Medium	Medium	High-Low
Time	(Major)	Medium	High-Medium	High-Medium
Discomfort		Medium	Medium	Low
Inconvenience	(Lesser)	Medium	Medium	Medium-Low
Unreliability		Low	Medium	Medium
Accident	(Minor)	Low	Low	Medium

Table 7.7. Off-Peak Hour versus Rush-Hour Trip Costs

Trip Costs	(Relative Importance)	Rail Transit	Bus Transit	Auto
Money		—	—	Less
Time	(Major)	More	—	Less
Discomfort		Less	Less	(Less)
Inconvenience	(Lesser)	More	More	—
Unreliability		—	Less	Less
Accident	(Minor)	—	—	—

thus become somewhat less expensive on the average than they are during rush hours. With single-fare pricing, off-peak transit trips, though shorter, are no less expensive for the traveler than rush-hour trips.

The net effect of these changes in relative money, trip time, discomfort, and inconvenience costs is to put all transit, and especially rail transit, at a substantial competitive disadvantage in the off-peak urban transportation market. It explains what is in any case obvious from the figures on transit riding already discussed. It also helps explain the difficulties that planners and transportation engineers face in trying to promote rail transit as an alternative to automobile transportation. Essentially, rail transit is well-suited only for rush-hour trips oriented to large concentrations of employment, that is, the CBD of large urban areas. These trips constitute only a small part of the present demand for urban

transportation.[13]   Given transit in its present form, moreover,
these trips are not likely to increase significantly.   Chapter 8 will
explore this problem further.

7.3 Estimating Transit Demand

Quite aside from the question of how transit can better serve our
urban areas in the future, planners and transportation engineers
must always confront the practical question of how to estimate the
demand that will actually materialize if some form of transit is
made available in an urban transportation market. As suggested
at the outset of this chapter, our ability to make such estimates is
seriously limited.

Several different methodological approaches to estimating transit
demand are in common use.   These break down roughly as below:

I. Direct Forecasting
II. Modal Split
  A. Direct factor:
    1. Pittsburgh Area Transportation Study (and others).
    2. Transit-use factor.
    3. Adams.
  B. Diversion curves.
  C. Traffic Research Corporation modal split.

Each of these approaches attempts to "model"—at least in part—the
mechanism of the urban transportation market.

The first of these, the direct-forecasting approach involves estimating transit trips directly from basic factors such as automobile ownership and residential density.   This approach ignores
questions of the relative cost (in the total sense discussed earlier)
of transit versus automobile trips.   It can take several forms. The
Pittsburgh Area Transportation Study, for instance, broke the
transit market down into (1) trips to the CBD, (2) school trips, and
(3) other trips.   While transit trips in the first category were estimated as a percentage of all CBD trips, empirical data served as
a basis for estimating transit trips in the last two categories directly: school trips as a function of net residential density and
"other" trips as a function of automobile ownership and net residential density.   Figure 7.5 shows the relationships used in this study.[14]

---

[13] Meyer, Kain, and Wohl get to the heart of this matter in their
discussion of CBD cordon line traffic volumes.   The relatively
small existing market for high-capacity transit lines is made quite
clear. See John R. Meyer, John F. Kain, and Martin Wohl, Technology and Urban Transportation, A report prepared for the White
House Panel on Civilian Technology, July 1962, (mimeographed),
pp. 45 ff.

[14] See Arthur Schwartz, Forecasting Transit Use, Highway Research Board Bulletin 297, Washington, D. C., 1961, pp. 29 ff.

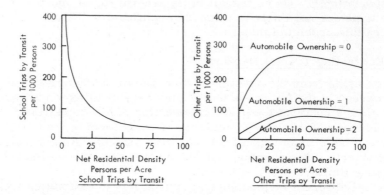

Figure 7.5. Transit trips versus residential density.
Source: B. V. Martin, F. W. Memmott, and A. J. Bone, Princi-
ples and Techniques of Predicting Future Demand for Urban Area Transportation, Research Report No. 38, M.I.T. Joint
Highway Research Project, Cambridge, 1961, p. 120.

By comparison, the Chicago Area Transportation Study estimated central-area transit trips on the basis of CBD land use and
concentration. Local trips were estimated on the basis of car
ownership per family.[15]   The factor of car ownership reflects, of
course, the constraints imposed upon the "captive" transit market
discussed in Section 7.1. The factor of land-use density reflects
the general trip-generating characteristics of an area; the assumption being that the way in which these trips split between modes also correlates closely with this same land-use factor.

The second method of approaching the transit demand problem
focuses entirely on this division of trips between competing modes
of transportation, that is, the "modal split." This approach pre-
supposes some independent technique of estimating the total number of trips that will be made by all modes in the study area.

The modal split has been determined in two ways, one of which
is similar to the direct forecasting of transit trips described immediately above. The Pittsburgh Area Transportation Study, for
instance, estimated the percentage of total CBD trips made by
transit on the basis of car ownership, net residential density, and
distance from the CBD.[16]   This is little different than estimating
transit trips directly from such factors. (It would be no different
if the estimate of total trips were based on the same factors; but
generally it is not.) The concept of a "transit-use factor" is a
variant of this same approach. To obtain this factor, population

---

[15] Chicago Area Transportation Study, Final Report, Vol. 2,
Chicago, 1960, pp. 58-69.
[16] Schwartz, Forecasting Transit Use, p. 29.

density is divided by car ownership.[17]   Figure 7.6 shows the relationship between modal split and transit-use factor.

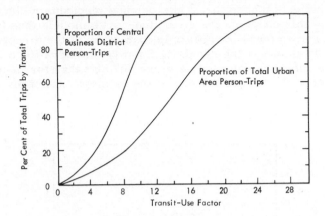

Figure 7.6. Transit-use curves.
Source: Wilbur Smith and Associates, Future Highways and
Urban Growth, New Haven, 1960, p. 130.

These approaches to the modal-split problem are relatively
crude, of course, because they consider only two or three of the
basic factors affecting the structure of the market. Warren T. Adams of the U. S. Bureau of Public Roads attempted a more elaborate model within the framework of the same direct-factor approach.
He has used multiple-regression techniques in analyzing data from
sixteen cities to find the relationship between modal split (for all
types of trips) and about a dozen basic factors descriptive of land
use, car ownership, and the concentration of transit service. The
resulting semilog equation is unwieldy, however, and may prove to
have limited practical value.[18]
The use of diversion curves constitutes a different approach to

[17] The concept is that of Wilbur Smith and Associates, who define
transit-use factor as below:

TUF = (1/1000)(households/automobile)(area population density)

An area with a population density of 10,000 people per square mile
and an average of one car per household would thus have a TUF =
10. See Wilbur Smith and Associates, Future Highways, p. 130.

[18] One might also question the conceptual basis of Adams' equation. The effort is a significant one, nonetheless, and hopefully
presages the development of better forecasting models than are
now available. See Warren T. Adams, Factors Influencing Transit
and Automobile Use in Urban Areas, Highway Research Board Bulletin 230 Washington, D. C., 1959, pp. 102 ff.

modal-split prediction. This approach focuses on the relative time cost of transportation to the users rather than upon the trip-producing characteristics of the area and the population served. While the approach reflects more closely the demand mechanism discussed in Section 2 of this chapter, the diversion-curve models thus far developed are even more over-simple than many of the direct-factor models. Determining the requisite input parameters for a diversion-curve approach can also be more difficult than for many direct-factor models.[19]   Figure 7.7 shows the principal set of diversion

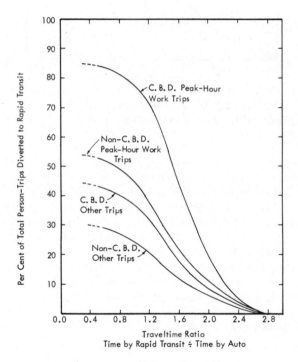

Figure 7.7. Rapid transit traffic diversion curves.
Source: Henry D. Quinby, "Traffic Distribution Forecasts—Highway and Transit," Traffic Engineering, February 1961, p. 27.

---

[19] The use of diversion curves for modal-split prediction has grown out of their use for predicting a driver's choice of route in highway traffic estimation. While they have been used with some success in route-choice prediction, there is reason to be skeptical about their suitability for modal-choice prediction. Too many factors other than traveltime seem important in modal choice.

curves developed for the San Francisco Bay Area Rapid Transit Study.[20]   Similar curves have been developed by studies in Chicago, Toronto, Washington, D. C., and other cities.

The Traffic Research Corporation of Toronto (TRC) has developed still another approach to the prediction of transit usage. The last of the operational (as opposed to strictly research) approaches we will mention specifically, it is the one that reflects most closely the essential mechanism of urban transportation demand. The approach determines modal split on the basis of the difference between automobile and transit trip costs with respect to three cost dimensions:

1. Traveltime;
2. Travel cost (weighted to account for differences in travelers' income levels);
3. Quality of service (inconvenience).

In effect, these three factors are the same as the first, second, and fourth factors we have included in the qualitative cost model of Tables 7.6 and 7.7. Only two slight differences should be noted. First, the TRC model recognizes that money does not have a strictly constant value and weights relative money costs by income level. Second, it uses waiting, transfer, and walking time as a measure of inconvenience, rather than as part of total trip time.

The TRC model has been programmed for solution by computer as part of an over-all traffic estimation and assignment model which has been applied in the Toronto Metropolitan Area.[21]   Figure 7.8 shows one set of the TRC modal split curves as used in Toronto. These are for work trips made by travelers with a "low economic indicator." A similar set was used for travelers with a high economic indicator. The model as programmed adjusts this factor to reflect relative travel cost. The results obtained with this approach have been good.

Many other ways of estimating transit trips have been attempted. The various approaches described earlier (but not necessarily the precise numbers shown in the figures) probably represent the best of current practice. Which approach a planner or engineer should use depends upon his confidence in the applicability of the underlying

---

[20] See Henry D. Quinby,   "Traffic Distribution Forecasts—Highway and Transit," Traffic Engineering, Vol. 31, No. 5, February 1961, pp. 22 ff.

[21] See D. M. Hill and Norman Dodd, Travel Mode Split in Assignment Programs,   Paper presented to the Origin and Destination Survey Committee of the Highway Research Board, Washington, D. C., January 1962.

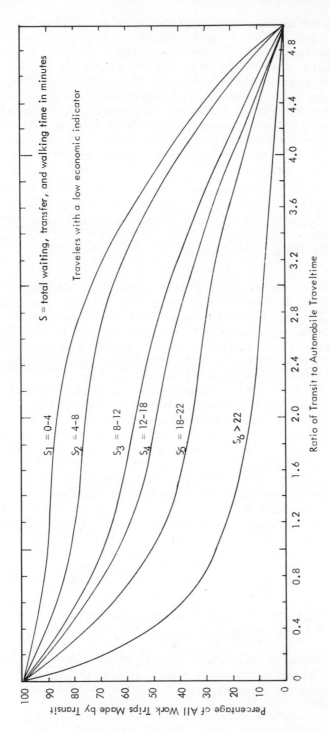

Figure 7.8. Transit share of work trips related to ratio of transit to automobile traveltime.
Source: D. M. Hill and Norman Dodd, Travel Mode Split in Assignment Programs, Paper presented at the Highway Research Board Annual Meeting, Washington, D. C., 1962.

relationships to his specific situation, as well as upon the raw data which are available. [22]

Fortunately, additional research into the general problem of modal choice is underway and should soon increase our ability to predict transit usage. Stanley L. Warner's work for The Transportation Center at Northwestern University is particularly interesting.
He has used advanced statistical techniques to investigate the way
in which relative time cost, relative money cost, and trip-taker's
income level affect the probability that one mode will be preferred
to another. This work was not intended to produce results that
were operational. It does point out, however, that relative time
and money cost are in fact important in explaining modal choice.
It found the effect of income to be less so. Further work on this
project may produce the most refined technique yet for predicting
transit demand. [23]

This type of research can eventually be helpful in still another
way. The forecasting techniques previously discussed are not only less than satisfactory in predicting demand for new transit lines,
they are virtually useless in predicting how the market will react
to changes in transit technology or in the type and quality of service offered on existing rail transit lines. Since the parameters
used in all of the present approaches are based upon data relating
to existing operations, the approaches themselves offer little basis
for predictions about the over-all future of rail transit as a mode
of transportation. Without the benefit of such refined research on
transit demand, we can merely suggest in the last chapter the general trends in transit usage that might result from certain possible
changes in design, operation, or public policies.

---

[22] For a good general description of many of these various methods, see B. V. Martin, F. W. Memmott, and A. J. Bone, Princi-
ples and Techniques of Predicting Future Demand for Urban Area
Transportation, Research Report No. 38, M. I. T. Joint Highway
Research Project, Cambridge, 1961, pp. 115-125.

[23] See Stanley L. Warner, Stochastic Choice of Mode in Urban
Travel, Paper prepared at The Transportation Center, Evanston,
Illinois, 1961.

Chapter 8

THE FUTURE OF RAIL TRANSIT

8.1 The Need for Innovation in Rail Transit

The future market for rail transit turns not only upon the emerg-
ing characteristics of our urban areas but also upon the developing
capabilities of various modes of urban transportation. In neither
respect are the directions entirely clear; but the case for rail transit in the years immediately ahead still seems in many ways predictable.

Certainly the geographic dispersal of our cities will continue
throughout the foreseeable future. Though more high-rise residential buildings may appear near city centers, it appears doubtful
that these will affect the proliferation of single-family dwellings in
the suburbs. Thus, over-all net residential densities will probably go steadily down in our older metropolitan areas, while in our
newer cities they will remain near their already low levels. Although more high-rise commercial buildings will also appear in or
near the CBD's of metropolitan areas, ratios of floor area per
worker, more off-street parking, and possible increases in urban
open space will keep commercial population densities near present
levels.[1]

In their recent study, Meyer, Kain, and Wohl suggest that the decentralization of our urban areas derives from fundamental changes
in technology, income levels, and consumer tastes, and would
take place independently of any public policy influences. They further suggest that with the exception of New York and possibly one
or two other major cities, the forces creating urban decentralization are significantly stronger than those favoring growth in central cities.[2]

The important thing is that this continuing pattern of development

---

[1] As an example of this trend, the prediction for Chicago in 1980
is a land-use and population-density pattern differing from the present largely in its higher percentage of land devoted to residential
use and in its significantly lower residential density. See Chicago
Area Transportation Study, Final Report, Vol. 2, Chicago, 1960,
p. 31.

[2] J. R. Meyer, J. F. Kain and M. Wohl, Technology and Urban
Transportation, A report prepared for the White House Panel on
Civilian Technology, July 1962, (mimeographed), pp. 3-10.

106

will add much to the decentralized, unstructured part of the urban transportation market and relatively little to the centralized and structured part. Social trips and non-CBD-oriented work and shopping trips will grow in number, while the regular flow of daily trips to central or satellite business districts will barely hold its own. At best, CBD trips will merely get longer as average commuting distances increase. Thus, in Chicago the prediction is that total CBD-oriented trips will increase only a few per cent over the next two decades, while total trips throughout the metropolitan area grow by a healthy 77 per cent.[3]

During the next few years the technology available to serve this urban market may change only slightly from our present technology. This derives from the inherent physical limitations of auto-highway, bus-highway, and rapid transit systems. Ultimately major departures from this conventional technology may appear, of course, because the market will probably demand them.

The automobile has long since proved its versatility as a means of urban transportation. It seems destined for an increasingly important role in the future, though from a technical standpoint it may change only marginally. The RAND study of urban transportation, after considering the technological future of the automobile in detail, concludes that by 1970 it will be lighter, a bit smaller, more comfortable, and a bit more economical of fuel—but it will be essentially the same automobile we know today.[4] That is, with one qualification: Should an efficient and inexpensive electric storage device appear, its over-all effect upon the competitive capabilities of the automobile might be profound. Such a development could permit major reductions in vehicle size and weight, maintenance expense, and fuel costs. These, along with many other possible benefits, would give the automobile an even greater edge over its urban competition than it now enjoys.

Public transportation will also be improving; but whether this will be at a rate sufficient for it to keep up with the automobile is questionable. Hoffman feels that even a moderate rate of automobile development will probably put private transportation even further ahead than it now is.[5] The bus, of course, should improve technologically at approximately the same rate as the automobile. Thus, it should also become more comfortable and less expensive. The cost improvement (barring the unlikely possibility of extensive automation) will be relatively smaller, however, since the heavy labor component of total bus-operating costs will be largely

---

[3] Chicago Area Transportation Study, Final Report, Vol. 2, Chicago, 1960, pp. 47, 60.

[4] See George A. Hoffman, The Automobile Today and Tomorrow, Paper Presented at the Annual Meeting of the Highway Research Board, Washington, D. C., January 9, 1962.

[5] Ibid., p. 26.

unaffected. (Private automobile operation, of course, involves essentially zero labor cost.) The net result may thus be a slightly weaker competitive condition for bus operations.[6]

In the face of even moderate technological advance by its competitors, rail transit must improve drastically if it is to hold its own, let alone make any substantial penetration into the increasingly unfavorable urban market. Probably no one type of innovation can bring this about. Just a reduction in the money cost of transit trips, no matter how significant, might have only a small effect upon this market. Research under way at the Transportation Center suggests that the market for all urban transportation may in fact be quite unresponsive to reductions in money cost.

Reductions in time costs may be limited in their effectiveness, too. As Chapter 7 points out, much of the trip time spent by transit riders depends upon the geographical dispersion of trip ends and is thus beyond the influence of transit technology or operating policies. The necessity for intermediate station stops, moreover, puts a physical constraint on reductions in that portion of total trip time that is under control of the transit system. Only if trip-time reductions were coupled with reductions in traveler discomfort and inconvenience could rail transit force a wedge into the overall market; and even then money costs would have to hold in line.

One can conclude, therefore, that rail transit has the following needs in innovation. First, ways must be found to stem the rise in money cost to the passenger. Chapter 6 has suggested that for new systems this means a reduction in the capital cost of fixed construction. For existing systems whose capital costs have been largely written off, this means a reduction in operating costs. For either new or existing systems—but particularly for new ones—the only alternative to such innovation may be subsidy. In addition, ways must be found to keep trip times low on both new and existing systems—by using higher performance equipment, for instance, or by lengthening station spacings. At the same time, equipment should be made more comfortable and service somehow made more convenient.

The remainder of this chapter deals briefly with the possibilities and the problems associated with these innovation needs.

8.2 The Impact of Improved Technology

In judging the possible impact of new technology upon rail transit, it is useful to think in terms of four different areas. The first

---

[6] Despite any disadvantage in technological development potential, the bus may yet achieve greater competitive standing in the total urban transportation market. A number of students of urban transportation have pointed this out. See report of Meyer, Kain, and Wohl.

three follow the general breakdown made earlier in this work: supporting way (including signals), stations and terminals, and equipment. The fourth, "automation," is in a category by itself.

Innovations in the first of these areas, the supporting way, will be steady, but their net effect upon rail transit as a means of urban transportation may be largely unimportant. The track structure itself is a case in point. More welded rail, more permanent-maintenance track construction, and more mechanized maintenance practices will all serve to bring track costs down and track quality up. Yet track accounts for a very small part of first costs and only about 10 per cent of operating costs, so that even more radical changes than those suggested would have little effect upon the competitive strength of a system from the standpoint of money costs. From the standpoint of quality there also seems little to gain. Better-riding and more reliable track will be little noticed by the average passenger.

Also insignificant from the cost standpoint, but perhaps important from the standpoint of both passenger comfort and general public acceptance, is the possibility of track designs that will reduce operating noise levels. Welded rail answers much of the noise problem, but more could be done to help damp out present track noise.

Improvements in signaling also fall in the marginal category with respect to their net effect upon transit capabilities. Though signaling systems can ultimately become entirely automatic, they now account for little more than 2 or 3 per cent of operating costs and thus can save relatively little. The increase in track capacity which such improvements permit could be more important, particularly on some existing lines whose capacity is now overtaxed.[7]

Advances in underground construction techniques could have a more significant effect. As has been shown, the carrying charges on tunnel construction costs are by far the most important single element in total transit money costs. Further development of the large cutting machines now in use on special tunneling applications might drastically reduce the cost of deep subway tubes. The prospects are less good for cut-and-cover construction, where the difficult problem of relocating underground utilities becomes more serious each year. Finding the key to that problem might in itself be a major contribution toward lower transit costs.

The development of elevated structures which are aesthetically acceptable in densely built-up downtown areas is the one improvement to the supporting way that seems of major potential

---

[7] One must recall in this respect, however, the relatively small number of urban corridors demanding or likely to demand carrying capacities in excess of those provided by conventional transit technology. See the discussion of this in Chapter 5 and the report of Meyer, Kain, and Wohl.

significance. Using elevated rather than subway construction could conceivably reduce capital costs by $10 million per mile and thus cut total money costs per passenger-mile in half. Some of the designs already proposed but not yet tried (see Figure 2.1, for instance) might even meet this aesthetic requirement. Unfortunately we have little experience to draw on in this highly subjective (and thus relatively unpredictable) problem. Our old elevated steel structures were and are today quite unacceptable, but we have yet to give newer structural concepts an opportunity.[8] Despite this lack of an adequate test to date, there is no cause for great optimism about elevated structures. Any structure sited above a city street will cause aesthetic interference and thus be a probable source of public resistance.[9]

Significant innovations in stations or terminals seem even less likely than those in track or other fixed facilities. New building materials can improve the flow of passengers. New fare collection techniques can reduce the costs of operation. The cumulative effect of changes in these various respects would be to attract some patrons and eliminate some costs; but the net effect upon over-all transit capabilities would probably be small.

Innovations in equipment are in a different class because they can affect operating capabilities as well as passenger reactions much more directly. The possibilities for improvement, moreover, are quite good.

There seems little doubt, for example, that lower-weight equipment having adequate structural strength can and will be developed. It has already been pointed out that such weight reductions result in direct savings in power costs as well as in the costs of maintenance of way and structures.

An improvement in passenger comfort through better ventilation and the provision of better seating is also well within present technical capabilities. Actually improvements in these two respects can be complementary. Increasing the proportion of total passengers seated reduces the total passenger loadings in each car. With lower loadings the provision of satisfactory ventilation or air conditioning becomes a simpler problem.

---

[8] The only elevated transit structures of any significance built in recent years have been those designed for supported monorails (e.g., those at Disneyland and, more recently, in Seattle). Unfortunately, however, supported monorail structures probably have less potential aesthetic acceptability than the suspended type. This is important, because if monorail in any form has an advantage over conventional rail transit, it lies in the area of aesthetic acceptability alone. See Botzow, Monorails (New York: Simmons-Boardman Books, 1960).

[9] An interesting but inconclusive analysis of this problem appears in City and Suburban Travel, No. 50, May 1962, pp. 8-10.

Any reduction in peak-hour passenger loadings, of course, will aggravate the problem of high equipment costs. Rail transit is already at a disadvantage in this regard when compared to buses.[10] At the same time, reductions in the capital cost of equipment seem very much in sight. These will occur partly as a result of reductions in car weight. The use of articulated vehicles (that is, a three-car unit mounted on four trucks instead of six) could also contribute importantly to the reduction of car costs.[11]

8.3 The Impact of Automation

The automation of rail transit operations must be counted as a possible innovation of some significance. It is a mistake to assume, however, that this innovation in itself can transform rail transit into an overpowering competitor in the urban transportation market. The following discussion makes this clear.

Two major aspects of transit operations are subject to wholesale automation: train operation and fare collection. The automation of train operation has received the most attention and from a cost and service standpoint is more important. The technical problems associated with developing adequate train-control equipment are challenging in detail, but there is no aspect of the over-all problem which existing technology and technical know-how cannot handle. Any number of experimental crewless trains (both railway and transit) have been run during the past few years. Most recently, of course, the New York City Transit Authority has inaugurated an automated shuttle train in regular service. While this operation is simple compared to a typical multistop line, the automated shuttle is a valid demonstration of the practicability of crewless operation. A very thorny labor relations problem involving the motormen and guards displaced by automation remains, however, and at this writing the NYTCA has not yet found an answer to it. This problem could presumably be avoided altogether in the case of a newly constructed line.

---

[10] Meyer, Kain, and Wohl point out that a 53-passenger bus with 4.8 square feet of floor space per seat (i.e., $K = 0.21$ passenger per square foot) costs only $630 per seat. Using the same standard, a $77,500 rail transit car with 380 square feet of floor space would seat 79 passengers; but even at the low cost of $77,500 this would be $980 per seat. The economic life of the transit car is admittedly longer, but the higher potential utilization of bus seats may offset that advantage.

[11] Mr. Alan R. Cripe of the Reynolds Metal Company in a letter to the authors dated July 2, 1962, further suggests that the use of gas turbine vehicles with high-frequency a-c generator-motor systems now seem feasible. These vehicles could be used for low to medium density operations, thus avoiding the capital cost of fixed electrification.

The economic effects of crewless train operation are important.
Table 6.7 suggests that conducting transportation characteristically accounts for about 45 per cent of the total costs of operation and
maintenance. Section 6.4 points out that the pay of motormen and
guards in turn accounts for but 30 to 40 per cent of the cost of conducting transportation. Thus, some 15 to 20 per cent of total operating and maintenance cost is susceptible to this type of automation at most. The maximum figure must be tempered in other
ways. First, there is a possibility (as discussed in Chapter 4)
that public pressure would demand an attendant of some sort on every train, even though he is not required for its operation. Second, the automated control equipment would in itself cost money
to install and maintain. The net effect of these requirements could
be to reduce the maximum expected benefit to about 10 to 15 per
cent of operating and maintenance costs.

The effect of crewless train operation upon the total money cost
of rail transit transportation depends further upon the capital costs
of the system. In the case of an existing system whose capital
costs have been partly or wholly written off or are subsidized in
some way, the 10 to 15 per cent saving would carry through almost
entirely to the total money costs. In the case of a new transit system, however, the 10 to 15 per cent would be reduced by the percentage of the total cost that was attributable to capital costs. Figure 6.3 suggests this might be anywhere from 50 to 80 per cent.
Thus, the net effect of automating train operations on a new facility may be 3 to 7 per cent of total money costs. The discussion in
Chapter 7 makes it clear that from a competitive standpoint, a 10
to 15 per cent reduction in total money cost is rather insignificant.
A 3 to 7 per cent reduction is that much more so.

Emphasizing money cost alone overlooks another important advantage of crewless operation discussed in Chapter 4: the ability
to provide frequent off-peak hour service at no increase in cost.
This would help overcome one of the major service disadvantages
of low-density (and thus high-cost) systems in particular. To the
extent this served to recapture off-peak traffic, it would have the
further effect of reducing over-all unit costs per passenger-mile,
because the heavy burden of fixed costs would then be spread over
a larger number of rides.

Again, there is some question about how significant this improvement would be. As Chapter 7 has pointed out, the long-run shift
in the trip-making characteristics of urban populations will still
conspire more and more against rail transit riding during off-
peak hours.

Fare collection is the other major area in which automation can
make a definite improvement. We have discussed a number of
the relevant technical possibilities in Chapter 3; it remains here
to assess their competitive significance. In Section 6.4 we have
shown that station collectors account for 20 to 25 per cent of total

transportation costs. Referring again to Table 6.7, this means a-
bout 10 per cent of total operating and maintenance costs. How
much of this 10 per cent could actually be saved depends very much
upon the particular collection scheme adopted. For a scheme requiring manual checking the savings would be but a fraction of the
present cost, inasmuch as many transit stations already operate
with only one collector. For any scheme that eliminated manual
checking the cost of the rather sophisticated ticketing machines
required might offset most of the wage savings.

We would venture to guess, therefore, that no more than 5 per
cent of the total operating and maintenance cost would be saved by
automating the fare collection function. Following such reasoning,
this would be reduced to a saving of only 1 to 3 per cent in the total money cost of a newly constructed system, a competitively insignificant figure.

There are, of course, other areas where automation can produce
savings. Maintenance of equipment and maintenance of way both
qualify in this regard. Given their relatively smaller share of total costs and their lower labor cost components, however, even
the maximum automation of these maintenance functions can produce only minor improvements in over-all rail transit performance.

In summary, automation in its various forms can improve rail
transit operations markedly; but it cannot be expected to work
wonders. Under present practices labor costs account for about
70 per cent of total operating and maintenance costs. This suggests that probably no more than 50 per cent of the total operating
and maintenance costs might be in any way susceptible to elimination. The cost of automation would further reduce the potential
savings to perhaps 30 to 35 per cent of present costs. For new
systems with their heavy burden of fixed costs, this saving may
finally reduce to a maximum of 15 per cent of total money costs.
Given the other competitive disadvantages of the average rail transit system, this sort of cost saving may be helpful, but it will not
be in any way decisive.

8.4 Meeting the Financial Needs of Rail Transit

The earlier sections of this chapter have cast some doubt on the
help that rail transit can expect in the near future from technological improvement alone. Despite such predictions, many planners
and engineers would still be unwilling to give up the notion of expanded rail transit systems as a partial solution to the transportation problems, real or imagined, which presently plague our metropolitan areas. This raises the question of whether cities ought
not to furnish their rail transit systems, present or future, with
direct financial help in the form of subsidy. Though we cannot
and will not attempt to settle this question here, it seems appropriate to discuss it briefly before leaving the subject of the future
of rail transit.

Subsidy is generally used as a device to lower the price of rail transit services and thus stimulate the aggregate demand for these services.[12]   In this context it is of interest to note at least two of the alternative policies which might be followed in pricing rail transit services.

The first of these is "average cost pricing," a policy whereby fares are established to cover the full costs of providing the transit service.   (This is in theory the policy that regulatory agencies sometimes follow in governing the fare structure of private transit companies.   In this case, full costs are considered to include a reasonable allowance for profit.)   There may be no fare level, however, that satisfies this condition.   That is to say, there may not be a traffic volume at which the resulting average costs are as low as the fare necessary to attract that traffic volume.   This situation is typical of some present rail transit operations and has made their subsidization necessary.

A second alternative is what might be called "consumer surplus pricing," a policy designed to produce a net subsidizable loss approximately equal to the added benefits realized by those riders willing to pay higher fares than those actually charged.   The resulting size of the justifiable subsidy bears no necessary relation to fixed charges, operating and maintenance expense, or any other single component of transit system costs.   While a community may actually be looking for other benefits from a program of transit subsidy, moreover, consumer surplus benefits accrue only to the riders who use the system.

It is arguable at best whether others may also benefit from such subsidization of rail transit.   Some writers suggest, for instance, that diverting trips from crowded highways to transit may—under the right circumstances—result in some increase in net consumer surplus, at least in the short run.   It is unlikely that any general endorsement of this particular subsidy argument is justified.

The difficulty here is that this same consumer surplus argument can be used as justification for the subsidization of any transportation facility—or any other economic activity, for that matter! That is, one could justify subsidizing highway users (e.g., by reducing the gas tax) on the grounds that many users would actually pay more to use the highway system than they now pay, that to this extent the highways would be generating a greater net consumer surplus if they were subsidized, and that one could justify spending that greater net amount in subsidy before producing any total disbenefit to the economy.

The fundamental issue is whether public transit should receive

---

[12] Instances can be found wherein the real motivation for subsidy was merely to effect a transfer of income from the taxpayer to the transit rider.

a "special dispensation" allowing it to capture consumer surplus in this way when no other activity is allowed to do so. In particular, one should note that capital investments in the private sector cannot rely upon consumer surplus for their justification in any way. Economic efficiency in the use of capital suggests that investments in the public sector should compete on the same terms.

A decision to subsidize rail transit should depend, of course, upon social and political goals as well as upon whether any indirect economic benefits to society as a whole can be considered significant.[13] These are questions beyond the scope of this study.

---

[13] See, for example, A. G. Pool, "The Subsidizing of Public Transport," Journal of the Institute of Transport, Vol. 28, No. 12, September 1960, pp. 365 ff.

SOME CONSIDERATIONS OF MINIMUM HEADWAY

A.1 Theoretical Minimum Headway

In determining the minimum headway possible between trains operating over a single track it is useful to consider the theoretical minimum which would be possible if practical difficulties were neglected. In Figure A.1, time-distance relationships for the rear

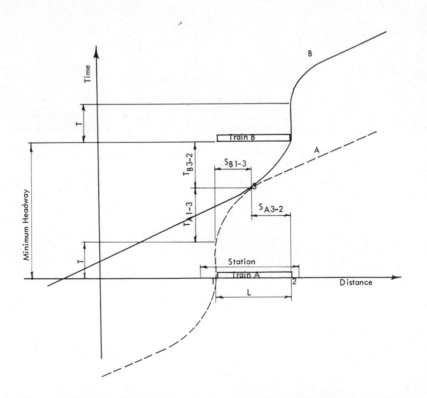

Figure A.1. Minimum theoretical headway.

end of Train A and the front end of Train B are shown by the curves labeled A and B, respectively. The minimum theoretical headway is given by the time that elapses from the moment the front of Train B arrives at the same point.

Figure A.1 shows that the minimum theoretical headway occurs when the time-distance curves are tangent. (Intersection of the curves would indicate a rear-end collision.) At this point of tangency, the slopes of the two curves are the same; that is, the speed of Trains A and B are equal.

If we assume acceleration and deceleration rates to be the same, the following observations can be made. The distance Train B travels (denoted by S_{B1-3}) in decreasing from its entering speed at Point 1 (V_{B1}) to its speed at the point of tangency (V_{B3}) is equal to the distance Train A travels in increasing from its speed at the point of tangency (V_{A3}) to its leaving speed at Point 2 (V_{A2}). In other words,

$$S_{A3-2} = S_{B1-3} = L/2$$

Then from symmetry,

$$t_{A1-3} = t_{B3-2}$$

If the station stop time is denoted as T, minimum theoretical headway is given by the equation

$$h = T + t_{A1-3} + t_{B3-2} = T + 2t_{A1-3}$$

where

$$h = \text{headway in seconds}$$

The time required for the rear of Train A to travel a distance equal to one-half its length (from Point 1 to Point 3) is given by the equations of motion as $\sqrt{2(L/2)/a}$ or $\sqrt{L/a}$. Thus, the expression above reduces to

$$h = T + 2\sqrt{\frac{L}{a}} \qquad (A.1)$$

A.2 Minimum Headway with Wayside Signals

At an early stage in the history of rapid transit operations, signaling techniques were developed to provide adequate protection against rear-end collisions between trains. These signal systems, which have already been described in Chapter 2, incorporate methods through which each train is informed of the track condition ahead.

On nearly all rapid transit lines, a "three-block clearing" signal system is used in order to make use of the automatic train-stop referred to in Chapter 2. Under this system, two signals behind each train display a red aspect, while the third and fourth signals display yellow and green, respectively. The additional block (Block S3 in Figure A.2) is introduced so that a train can still come to a

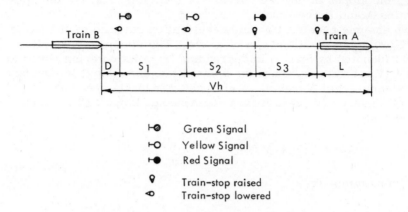

Figure A.2. Three-block clearing headway, no station stop.

safe stop in the event it passes a red signal (Signal 3 in this case) at maximum speed. In Figure A.2, minimum headway is given without station stops by the equation

$$h = \frac{\sum_{}^{3} S_i + D + L}{V} \qquad (A.2)$$

where

S_i = length of Block i in feet
D = sighting distance to signal = Vt
t = signal equipment operating time plus time required for motorman's observation of the signal
V = speed of the train over the three blocks in feet per second

From this equation it follows that headway will be reduced as block lengths become shorter. These lengths cannot be less than the stopping distance required for a train entering each block, plus a margin of safety to allow for malfunction of train brakes or poor track condition. Block length with a 35 per cent safety factor is given by $1.35V_i^2/2d$, and Equation A.2 becomes

$$h = \frac{\frac{1.35}{2d}\sum_{}^{3} V_i^2 + D + L}{V} \qquad (A.2a)$$

where V_i^2 is maximum speed of a train entering Block i. Where no stops are to be made over three adjacent blocks, the equation for minimum headway reduces to

$$h = \frac{\frac{1.35}{2d}(3V^2) + Vt + L}{V}$$

$$= \frac{2.03V}{d} + t + \frac{L}{V} \tag{A.2b}$$

By holding d, L, and t constant, and differentiating with respect to V, minimum headway occurs when

$$\frac{dh}{dV} = \frac{2.03}{d} - \frac{L}{V^2} = 0$$

or

$$V_{cr.} = \sqrt{\frac{Ld}{2.03}} \tag{A.3}$$

where $V_{cr.}$ = critical speed for minimum headway. Any increase or decrease in train speed from this value will result in a decrease in the theoretical number of trains which can pass through this section in one hour.

It is more usual, however, for critical headway conditions to occur in sections where there are station stops.[1] In this case headways are increased because of the time required for acceleration and deceleration of the train as well as the time required for the station stop itself. This is indicated in Figure A.3. While Train A remains in the station, the following train would be required to stop at Signal 2 under a three-block clearing system. When Train A clears Signal 4, the following train may advance to Signal 3, but only after the leaving train has cleared Signal 5 will the automatic train-stop at Signal 3 clear so as to permit Train B to enter the station. However, since the train-stop at Signal 3 does not clear until Train A has cleared Signal 5, the following train must be sufficiently behind Signal 3 to be able to stop if required. In the case of a free-running condition, it must be almost at Signal 2. Minimum headway will then be given by the sum of the time required for Train A to leave the station and clear Signal 5, the time required for Train B to travel from Signal 2 to the stopping point in the station,

---

[1] A situation in which headways are limited by a section containing no stops might occur where two lines shared a section of track for a certain distance, and then diverged to separate tracks and stations.

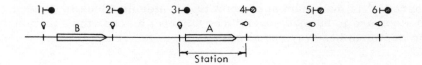

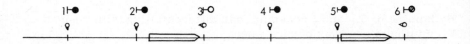

Figure A.3. Three-block clearing headway with station stop.

and the station stop time itself. The time required for Train A to leave is equal to the time required to accelerate to its leaving speed plus the time necessary to travel the remaining distance at its leaving speed. This is given by

$$\text{Leaving time (train A)} = \frac{V}{a} + \left(L + \frac{1.35V^2}{2d} - \frac{V^2}{2a}\right)\frac{1}{V}$$

while

$$\text{Entering time (train B)} = \frac{V}{d} + \left[\frac{2(1.35V^2)}{2d} - \frac{V^2}{2d}\right]\frac{1}{V}$$

$$= \frac{1.35V}{d} + \frac{V}{2d}$$

Then

$$h = \frac{V}{a} + (L + \frac{1.35V^2}{2d} - \frac{V^2}{2a})\frac{1}{V} + \frac{1.35V}{d} - \frac{V}{2d} + T$$

which reduces to

$$h = T + \frac{L}{V} + \frac{V}{2a} + \frac{5.05V}{2d} \tag{A.4}$$

This equation has been plotted in Figure A.4 for different values of speed, rate of acceleration, train length, and station stop time.

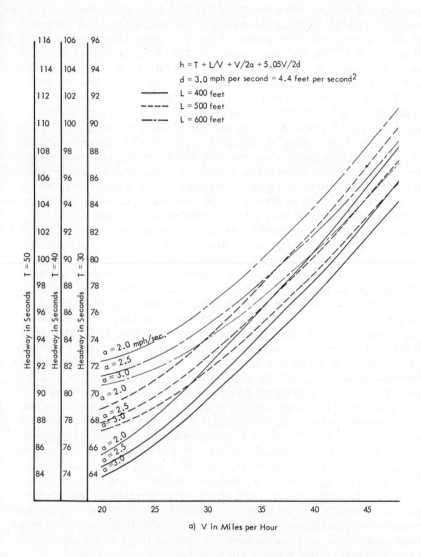

Figure A.4. Headway, speed, and capacity relationships.

A.3 Speed Control and Cab Signaling

One of the major disadvantages of this three-block clearing system as described here, is that, once block lengths have been established, trains are required to maintain minimum space intervals,
regardless of speed. For example, it has been assumed in the previous calculations that the following train would not enter Block 2
until the leaving train had passed Signal 5, thus clearing the train
stop at Signal 3. In the usual case, if Train B arrived at Signal 2
before this time, it would precede through Block 2 at reduced speed,
under a yellow signal, prepared to stop at Signal 3. During this
time, Train A may have passed Signal 5, thereby allowing Train B
to continue on into the station under a yellow aspect at Signal 3.
However, should Train A remain in the station too long, the following train would first stop at Signal 2, then accelerate and decelerate to the stopping point after receiving the proper clearance. In
order to reduce this time loss, speed control signals can be used
so that "trains approaching an occupied station might either keep
moving at a slow rate of speed or, if compelled to stop, might come
as close as possible to the station, consistent with safety." [2]

With speed control systems, deceleration of the following train
is controlled through a series of signals located in the approach
zone to a station and spaced at intervals of less than full stopping
distance. Successive signals are cleared by time relays, so that
trains moving at low speeds will not be stopped but those moving at
high speeds will. This permits a train approaching a station to
come closer to the train that is standing in the station by slacken-
ing its speed, though each signal clears only when the next signal
provides a protective braking distance between that signal and the
train ahead. Any reduction in headway resulting from this signaling method is obtained at the expense of average speed.

Determination of minimum headway under these conditions does
not lend itself to the analytical approach used previously in deriv-
ing the headway equations for normal three-block clearing conditions. By using a sufficiently large number of closing-in signals
and slow enough intermediate speeds, headways can be reduced to
a level almost entirely dependent upon the duration of the station
stop. Given the performance characteristics of the vehicle, the
duration of the station stop, and the desired headway, however,
graphical methods can be used to establish the location and number
of speed control signals. These will also show that minimum headway depends upon several factors, including train entering speed
and the location of the signals themselves.

A cab signal system is more readily analyzed. Under this type
of system a train may approach a preceding train as closely as desired after acknowledging that the lowest speed restriction is in

[2] M. Lynn Patterson, "Methods of Locating Automatic Signals,"
Railway Signal Engineer, Vol. 9, No. 2, February 1916.

effect. It can be shown that if a following train is to stop a minimum distance of "S" behind the preceding train, headway will be given by

$$h = T + 2\sqrt{\frac{L+S}{a}} + Y \qquad (A.5)$$

where

Y = time in seconds to permit motorman to acknowledge the overspeed alarm and take action

Comparing this equation with that for wayside signaling (Equation A.4) shows that the advantage of cab signaling increases with higher speeds.

A.4 Minimum Headway with Automation

Chapter 2 has already pointed out that automation may eliminate the need for maintaining safe stopping distances between successive trains. Under such a system the speed of a following train would be adjusted in accordance with the speed of the preceding train. If a train were forced to stop before entering the station because of a delay in the departure of the preceding train, minimum headway would then be similar to the values obtained with a cab signal system, as given by Equation A.5. Under the best conditions, however, headways should approach the theoretical minimum as given by Equation A.1, with some margin of safety to allow for communication between trains. Thus the minimum headway would be given by

$$h = T + 2\sqrt{\frac{L}{a}} + R \qquad (A.6)$$

where

R = communication time (in seconds)

A.5 Summary of Headway Equations

The following is a summary of the more important equations developed in this appendix. For wayside signal systems only the equation for simple, three-block clearing is given. It should be noted, however, that by reducing signal spacing through the introduction of speed control signals, the system approaches, in effect, a cab signal system (which may be considered a wayside system having an infinitesimal spacing between signals). In this case, minimum possible headways using wayside signals should be equivalent to those obtainable with cab signals.

Equation	Minimum Headway	Remarks
A.1	$T + 2\sqrt{\dfrac{L}{a}}$	Theoretical minimum neglecting practical considerations.
A.2b	$\dfrac{L}{V} + \dfrac{2.03V}{d} + t$	Wayside signals, assuming no stops, a critical speed of $Ld/2.03$, and a 35 per cent safety factor.
A.4	$T + \dfrac{L}{V} + \dfrac{V}{2a} + \dfrac{5.05V}{2d}$	Wayside signals, assuming a station section and a 35 per cent safety factor.
A.5	$T + 2\sqrt{\dfrac{L + S}{a}} + Y$	Cab signals, assuming the following train stops behind the preceding train before entering the station.
A.6	$T + 2\sqrt{\dfrac{L}{a}} + R$	Completely automated system.

Special References on Signaling

Ingmar Boberg, "Modern Signalling in New Subways in Stockholm, Sweden," Railway Signaling and Communications, Vol. 47, No. 3, March, 1954, pp. 38-44.

H. G. Brown, "The Signalling of a Rapid Transit Railway," Journal of the Institution of Electrical Engineers, Vol. 52, No. 223, May 1, 1914, pp. 545-553.

Chester Ross Davis, "Signal System, Interlocking Plants, and Automatic Train Control on the San Francisco-Oakland Bay Bridge Railway," Electrical Engineering, Vol. 59, No. 3, March 1940, pp. 158-164.

A. D. J. Forster, "The Capacity of Rapid Transit Railways." Paper read before the Sydney (Australia) University Engineering Society, November 29, 1918.

Robert C. Johnson, "A Scientific Method of Locating Automatic Block Signals for a Railroad of Heavy Traffic," Railway Signal Engineer, Vol. 15, Nos. 9 and 10, 1922.

M. Lynn Patterson, "Methods of Locating Automatic Signals," Railway Signal Engineer, Vol. 9, No. 2, February 1916.

"Speed Control in Interborough Subway," Electric Railway Journal, Vol. 66, No. 2, July 11, 1925, pp. 49-52.

J. M. Waldron, "Speed Control Signals," Journal of the Railway Signaling Association, 1910, pp. 161 ff.

Appendix B

DETERMINATION OF TRANSIT COSTS

B.1 Average and Incremental Costs

The important cost for analysis purposes is always the incremental and not the average cost. A simple example illustrates this point. In standard accounting methods it is usual to determine average costs by dividing the total cost of production (in this case, of transportation) by the quantity produced. In Figure B.1,

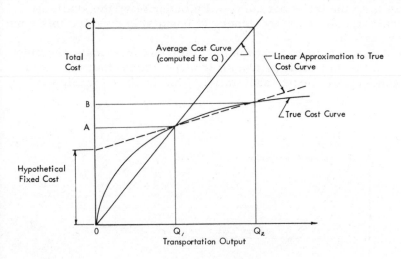

Figure B.1. Comparison of total average and incremental costs.

for instance, assume we know simply that Q_1 units of transportation were produced at a total cost of 0A. The average cost of transportation would then be given by $0A/Q_1$. In estimating the cost of producing Q_2 units of transportation, the use of this average cost would lead to the value 0C. Actually, the true cost as shown here should be only 0B, since the true cost curve (as is usual) does not coincide with the average cost curve because of the economies of increasing scale of operation. In order to estimate the cost at an output such as Q_2 correctly, it would thus be necessary to know either the shape of the true cost curve or the incremental cost AB at a level of output equal to Q_1.

125

Rail transit companies do not have readily available either incremental costs or true cost curves for maintenance and operation. The available cost data are largely average costs as determined by standard accounting procedures established primarily to assist public utilities commissions in establishing fare schedules. For analysis purposes such data can leave much to be desired, as the previous example indicates.

Using such data as are available to determine true cost curves is also difficult. The annual transportation output for a rail transit property usually varies only slightly over any period of time for which costs remain comparable. In examining the associated cost data, one can develop only the portion of the cost curve that relates to this restricted range of output. If, for example, a property had in the past produced between Q_1 and Q_2 units of output annually, only that part of the cost curve between Q_1 and Q_2 would be known. Within these limits, however, a straight line drawn through these two points (see Figure B.1) might represent a reasonably good approximation to the true cost curve. Unfortunately, the available data on rail transit costs are generally unsuitable even for this sort of approximation.

These same differences between average and true costs are also reflected in the unit costs of transit transportation—that is, costs per passenger-mile or per seat-mile. This is shown in Figure B.2,

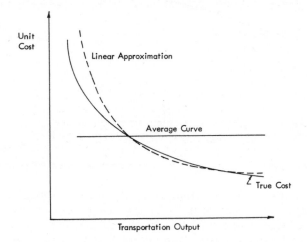

Figure B.2. Comparison of unit average and incremental costs.

where the total costs in Figure B.1 have been transformed into unit costs. All existing data on transit unit costs (including those in this book) must be interpreted with this in mind.

B.2 A Rail Transit Cost Model

As suggested at the outset of Chapter 6, it is convenient to deal
with costs in terms of their fixed and variable components. In a
rail transit system the interest and depreciation on the investment
in fixed property (track and supporting structures, stations, power
supply and distribution systems, signaling and communication systems, etc.) constitute the "fixed" component of total cost. These
costs generally remain constant for a fairly wide range of system
capacities, except in the very long run. Characteristically it is only when capacity is to be increased (or decreased) well beyond this
range that these fixed investment costs will change. Since investment to increase capacity can involve such major items as the addition of tracks or the replacement of a signal system, the level of
fixed costs associated with capacity will generally follow some form
of step function. This is shown in Figure B.3, where the costs of
carrying the investment in fixed property are represented by E_F.

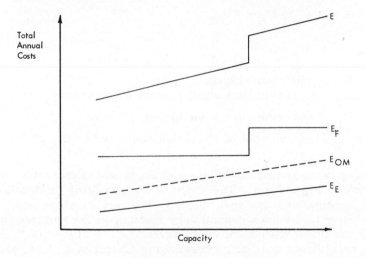

Figure B.3.   Total annual costs as a function of capacity.

Interest and depreciation on the investment in equipment constitute an intermediate type of cost for a rail transit system; a cost
which in the short run is fixed, but in the longer run is essentially
variable. While the transit operator is interested in both of these
possibilities, the planner and design engineer are particularly interested in the long-run situation. In this context, any increase in
peak-hour capacity implies an increase in equipment requirements—
assuming, as we will, that for any specified peak-hour capacity,
equipment requirements have been minimized as outlined in

Chapter 5. Thus, the costs associated with the ownership of equipment will go up when capacity is increased.[1] This is also shown in Figure B.3, where the costs of carrying the investment in equipment are represented as E_E.

The remaining costs of a rail transit system are those associated with its operation and maintenance; that is, those costs discussed in Sections 2 through 7 of Chapter 6. These are essentially variable (both in the short and long run) with changes in peak-hour capacity. As explained earlier in this chapter, a linear approximation to the true cost curve for operation and maintenance (in the usual range of capacities) would probably intercept the cost axis at some positive threshold cost. The plot of these variable costs in Figure B.3 suggests this, though in practice we are essentially limited to the use of average cost data and are thus unable to construct such a true cost curve.

Combining these three cost functions would yield a total annual cost function, represented in Figure B.3 as E. Thus

$$E = E_F + E_E + E_{OM}$$

where

E = total annual cost

E_F = carrying cost of permanent construction

E_E = carrying cost of equipment

E_{OM} = annual cost of operation and maintenance

Transforming these annual costs into unit costs would yield the curves shown in Figure B.4. The shape of the resulting total unit cost curve is completely general, though obviously its slope and position relative to the axes depend very much upon the relative importance of the three component cost curves.

With the rail transit cost data presented in Chapters 2, 3, 4, and 6, it is possible to evaluate these component cost curves in at least a general way. Given an approximate investment per route-mile in

---

[1] Notice that this proportional increase in ownership costs will actually hold true in both the short and the long run. Such would not generally be the case in a falling market situation. When peak-hour demands and thus equipment requirements decrease, it probably will not be possible to dispose of the resulting excess equipment in the short run except at some loss; it will be only in the long run that equipment investment costs can again be brought into line. On a graph of short-run costs, then, the equipment investment cost curve for a falling market would not be coincident with that for a rising market.

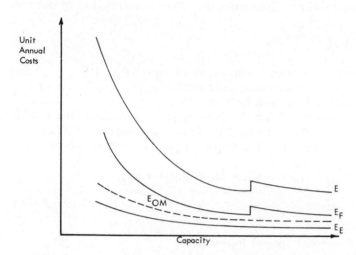

Figure B.4. Unit annual costs as a function of capacity.

fixed facilities, for instance, one can readily calculate their total annual cost. The same can be done for the equipment investment costs associated with various levels of peak-hour capacity, given some assumptions about equipment type, station spacing, and the number of round trips each car (or train) can make per rush hour. It is then straightforward to convert these annual costs to square feet of floor space per peak hour.

Calculation of operating and maintenance costs is less straightforward but not entirely impossible. Essentially this involves evaluating a relationship of the form

$$E_{OM} = K + Pu$$

where

E_{OM} = total annual cost of operation and maintenance at some specified level of peak-hour capacity
K = a constant threshold cost
P = total annual units of output (e. g., car-miles, ton-miles, etc.) associated with peak-hour capacity
u = total operation and maintenance cost per unit of output

Unfortunately there is no one measure of output (i. e., P in the previous equation) which is entirely satisfactory for use in such a relationship, nor (in line with the foregoing discussion of average

versus true cost curves) can we readily evaluate the constant term.
This forces us to use a somewhat different relationship of the form

$$E_{OM} = \sum_i P_i e_i$$

This considers more than a single output unit (P_1, P_2, . . .) and
the operating and maintenance cost variation (e_1, e_2, . . .) associated with each such output unit.

The figures developed for the five major cost categories in Chapter 6 are such that they can be fitted into this second relationship
reasonably well. In expanded form the equation then becomes

$$E_{OM} = (Tw + Ms + Mr + Tq)(1 + a)$$

where

> T = total annual ton-miles
> M = total annual car-miles
> w = maintenance of way and structures cost per
>   ton-mile
> s = maintenance of equipment cost per car-mile
> r = cost of conducting transportation per car-mile
> q = cost of electric power per ton-mile
> a = per cent of basic operating and maintenance
>   costs allocable to "other" operating expense

The estimation of total annual car-miles (M) in this equation involves assumptions about both peak- and off-peak-hour scheduling.
The peak-hour scheduling necessary to produce a given rush-hour
capacity follows readily from car size and train length. Off-peak-
hour scheduling is less predictable. In particular, policies on
maximum headway—a determinant of service quality in off-peak
hours—can differ widely. This is also true of policies on off-peak-
hour train length. Yet, for analysis purposes these differences
tend to wash out. As explained in Chapter 7, the time-distribution
of rider demand is very nearly the same from one property to another. An analysis of scheduling practices shows that car-mileage
also tends to split between peak and off-peak hours in a somewhat
constant ratio. Using such a ratio makes it possible to estimate
total annual car-miles directly from peak-hour car-miles.[2]

---

[2] This analysis assumes the rush (i.e., peak) hours run 4 hours
per working weekday, or (4 × 255) hours per year. The other 20
hours per working weekday, as well as all day Saturday, Sunday,
and holidays, are considered off-peak. On this basis, the following are the splits on traffic and car-miles in Toronto and Chicago.
A rough check for Cleveland yielded similar results.

(continued page 131)

Given an assumed car weight, an estimate of total annual ton-miles follows directly from that for car-miles.

B.3 Annual Route-Mile Cost: A Sample Computation

A. General Information (i.e., assumptions regarding facilities and costs)
   1. Performance data:
       Average speed including stops $\overline{V}$[1] = 25 miles per hour
       Minimum (rush-hour) headway (H) = 2 minutes
   2. Fixed plant (see Tables 2.1 and 3.3):
       Total cost per route-mile of double track, including stations, shops, and terminals = $15,000,000
       Expected life = 50 years[3]
   3. Equipment (see Table 4.2):[4]
       Size of cars (usable floor area) = 500 square feet

	Passengers		Car-Miles	
Transit Property	Peak	Off-Peak	Peak	Off-Peak
Toronto*	50%	50%	37	63
Chicago	47%	53%	37	63

*These car-miles have been recalculated on the basis of the actual Toronto schedule, but using shortened trains during the off-peak hours.

[3] There is some question as to the appropriate economic life to use in analyzing the costs of fixed transit facilities. Forty years is a usual figure for many types of public works. Certainly such things as rail, ties, ballast, signal system components, and the like will last no longer. It can be argued further that with the rapid change now taking place both in technology and in the patterns of economic activity, functional obsolescence will overtake almost any facilities within 40 years or less.

On the other hand, subway tubes once constructed will almost certainly continue to serve some useful purpose well beyond 40 years. Thus, one could argue that systems whose route-mile construction costs are very high should be accounted somewhat longer economic lives.

The choice of 50 years here is an attempt to compromise the resulting cost figures as best we can. The reader should recognize that in specific cases this may result in either an understatement or an overstatement of the carrying costs involved.

[4] The figures cited are not for any existing equipment, but represent the authors' estimate of what an "average" new car might be.

Cost per car = $90,000
Cost per unit of floor area = $450 pounds per square foot
Loaded car weight = 35 tons.
Loaded weight per unit of floor area = 140 pounds per
                                                    square foot
Expected life—25 years [5]

4. Operating and maintenance costs: [6]
   a. Way and structures (see Table 6.1):
      w = $2.50 per 1000 gross ton-miles
   b. Maintenance of equipment (see Table 6.2):
      s = $0.075 per car-mile
   c. Conducting transportation (see Table 6.3):
      r = $0.25 per car-mile
   d. Power (see Table 6.4):
      q = $2.00 per 1000 gross ton-miles
   e. Other operating expenses (see Table 6.5):
      a = 15 per cent of basic operating and maintenance
         costs

5. Rush-hour scheduling:

H (Rush-hour headway)	n (Cars per train)	J_r (Square-foot miles per mile per rush hour) $J_r = \frac{(60n)}{(H)}(500)$	P_k (Passengers per hour where k = 0.35)	P_k (Passengers per hour where k = 0.15)
4.0	4	30,000	10,500	4,500
3.0	6	60,000	21,000	9,000
2.0	6	90,000	31,500	13,500
2.0	8	120,000	42,000	18,000
2.0	10	150,000	52,500	22,500

B. Cost Computations
   Note: These computations assume an interest rate of 4 per
   cent as a conservative estimate of the cost of capital for

[5] Again there is a question as to the proper figure one should use
for economic life. Many would argue for lives of 30 years or more.
Some would argue that technological change will render new equipment obsolete in no more than 10 or 15 years, though a look at the
per car-mile maintenance costs in Table 6.2 suggests that this has
not happened with existing equipment.
   The choice of 25 years here is another attempt at compromise.
As with the figure for fixed facilities, the reader may feel this either understates or overstates the resulting carrying charges.
   [6] The authors have used conservative estimates of what an "average" transit company might do based on the cost information for
existing transit operations summarized in the various tables of
Chapter 6.

public projects.   The authors recognize that this may actually understate the true opportunity cost of capital, a problem
which is discussed briefly at the end of Chapter 6.

1. Annual carrying cost on fixed plant (E_F):

Capital recovery factor (4 per cent for 50 years) = 0.04655
$\overline{E_F}$ = (15,000,000)(0.04655) = \$698,250 per mile per year

2. Annual carrying costs on equipment (E_E):

Total number of cars required per route-mile (N)

$$N = (2)\frac{60n}{H\overline{V}^1} \qquad \text{(see Equation 5.2)}$$

Total equipment investment = \$90,000 N
Capital recovery factor (4 per cent for 25 years) = 0.06401
$\overline{E_E}$ = (90,000 N)(0.06401) = 5.760N

H (Rush-hour headway)	n (Cars per train)	N (Cars per route-mile)	$\overline{E_E}$ (Annual equipment cost per route-mile)
4.0	4	4.8	\$ 27,600
3.0	6	9.6	55,300
2.0	6	14.4	82,900
2.0	8	19.2	110,600
2.0	10	24.0	138,200

3. Annual operating and maintenance costs (E_{OM}):

Annual rush-hour car-miles per route-mile:

$$\overline{M}_R = (2)(\frac{60n}{H})(4)(255) = 122,400(\frac{n}{H})$$

Ratio of total annual car-miles to annual rush-hour car-
miles = 2.75 (see Section B.2)
Total annual car-miles per route-mile:

$$\overline{M} = 122,400 \, (\frac{n}{H})(2.75) = 336,000 \, (\frac{n}{H})$$

Total annual ton-miles per route-mile:

$$\overline{T} = 35 \, \overline{M} = 11,781,000 \, (\frac{n}{H})$$

4. Total annual costs per route-mile $(\overline{E})$:

$$\overline{E} = \overline{E}_F + \overline{E}_E + \overline{E}_{OM}$$

Square-Foot-Miles
   per Mile
 per Rush Hour   Annual Costs in $1000 per Route-Mile

(J_r)	$(\overline{E}_F)$	$(\overline{E}_E)$	$(\overline{E}_{OM})$	$(\overline{E})$
30,000	698.3	27.6	186.8	913
60,000	698.3	55.3	373.2	1127
90,000	698.3	82.9	560.4	1342
120,000	698.3	110.6	747.6	1557
150,000	698.3	138.2	933.6	1770

5. Unit cost per passenger-mile:
   The assumption here is that all cars are loaded during every rush-hour period at exactly the number indicated by the loading coefficient. Thus, total annual rush-hour passenger-miles = $(4)(255) \, P_k J_r = 1020 P_k J_r$

   Off-peak passenger-miles are assumed to be in the ratio of 50 to 50 (see Section B.2). Thus, total passenger miles = $1 + 50/50 = 2.00$ times rush-hour passenger-miles, or $2040 P_k J_r$.

Totals (000,000's omitted)   Total Annual Costs in $1000's per Route-Mile

H (Rush-hour headway)	n (Number of cars per train)	$\bar{M}$ (Annual car-miles per mile)	$\bar{T}$ (Annual ton-miles per mile)	W (M-of-w cost)	S (M-of-e cost)	R (Transportation cost)	Q (Power cost)	A (Other expense)	$\bar{E}_{OM}$ (Total o & m cost)
4	4	336.6	1180	29.6	25.2	84.0	23.6	24.4	186.8
3	6	673.2	23.56	58.8	50.4	168.0	47.2	48.8	373.2
2	6	1010.0	35.35	88.4	75.6	252.4	70.8	73.2	560.4
2	8	1340.4	47.12	118.0	100.8	336.8	94.4	97.6	747.6
2	10	1688.2	58.92	147.2	126.0	420.8	118.0	112.0	933.6

($k = 0.35$)

J_r (Square-foot-miles per mile per rush hour)	E (Total annual cost in $1000)	P_k (Passengers per hour)	Total Annual Passenger-Miles $\times 10^6$	Cost per Passenger-Mile
30,000	913	10,500	21.4	.043
60,000	1127	21,000	42.8	.026
90,000	1342	31,500	64.2	.021
120,000	1557	42,000	85.7	.018
150,000	1770	52,500	107.1	.017

($k = 0.15$)

P_k (Passengers per hour)	Total Annual Passenger-Miles $\times 10^6$	Cost per Passenger-Mile
4,500	9.2	.099
9,000	18.4	.061
13,500	27.5	.049
18,000	36.7	.042
22,500	45.9	.039

INDEX

Acceleration, factors influencing,
  42-44
  effect of rubber wheels, 55
Accidents, effect of automation, 57-58
  transit relative to other modes,
  97-98
Adams, Warren T., 101
Aesthetics of supporting structures,
  21-22
Air conditioning of vehicles, 52
Automation, effect on costs, 56-58,
  112-113
  effect on power consumption, 58
  effect on safety, 58
  effect on train headway, 67, 123
  of fare collection, 33-34
  impact of, 111-113
  New York City shuttle, 111
  of signal systems, 20-21
  of train operation, 56-58
Automobiles, costs of operation, 92n,
  93
  land requirements, 6
  public preference for, 6
  technological change, 107

Ballast, 15
Bello, Francis, 95n
Boberg, Ingmar, 124
Bolt Beranek and Newman, 22n, 54
Bone, A. J., 100, 105n
Botzow, H. S. D., 3n, 110n
Brown, H. G., 64n, 124

Capacity, 61-67
  calculations, 64-67
  determinants of, 61-64
  effect of automation on, 67
  effect on costs, 127-129
  effect of headway on, 121
  of passageways, 31
  of turnstiles, 33
  of vehicles, 46-51
Cars, transit, see Vehicles

Chicago Area Transportation Study,
  87, 89n, 90, 96n, 97n, 100,
  106n, 107n
Cleveland Transit System, 89n
Comfort, effect of rubber wheels on,
  54
  relation to capacity, 51
  of transit relative to other modes,
  96, 98
Construction, costs of, 23-25, 109
  methods, cut-and-cover, 11, 13
    ICANDA (Milan), 12, 15
    tunneling, 10-11
Consumer expenditures on transit, 5n
Controls for vehicles, 38
Costs, as affected by automation,
  56-58, 112-113
  automobile, 93
  comparative, 91-95
  of construction, 23-25
  of escalators, 35
  of stations, 35-36
  of transit operation, 68-84, 125-136
    average and incremental, 125-126
    conducting transportation, 72-74
    equipment maintenance, 40, 63-64
    interest, 82-83
    maintenance of way and structures,
      69-71
    other, 76
    power, 17, 40, 74-76
    relation to capacity, 78-82
    sample computations, 131-136
    total operating and maintenance,
      76-78
    transit cost model, 127-131
  of vehicles, 18, 47, 56, 58-60
    rubber-wheeled, 47, 56
Cripe, Alan R., 111n
Cross sections, cut-and-cover sub-
    ways, 14
  elevated structures, 10
  stations, 28, 29, 30
  tunnels, 12
Cut-and-cover construction, 11

---

*Underlined page numbers refer to illustrations; n following the page numbers
refers to footnotes.

137